SURPRISED BY THE SPIRIT

With warmest wishes

Charles

First published in 2020 by
New Life Publishing, Luton,
Bedfordshire LU4 9HG

© Charles Whitehead

British Library Cataloguing in Publication Data
A catalogue record for this book is available
from the British Library

Two photographs; pages 90 and 123 are included
© Servizio Fotografico Vaticano

ISBN   978 1 912237 22 7

Front cover photograph by Steve Murray
www.beholdmimeministry.org
and used with permission

Back cover 'Holy Spirit' by Yvonne Bell
www.vestments.co.uk
and used with permission

Typesetting by New Life Publishing,
Luton, UK www.goodnewsbooks.net
Printed and bound in Great Britain

SURPRISED
BY THE SPIRIT

MY PERSONAL STORY

Charles Whitehead

CONTENTS

Foreword, by David Payne 1

Introduction 3

1. The Story Begins 5

2. The Formative Years 15

3. A Perfect Partner 26

4. Life-Changing Moments 35

5. Praying Friends 40

6. A Grace for Us All 46

7. The Lord Speaks 54

8. Serving My Local Church Community 60

9. The Wider Community 75

10. International Catholic Charismatic
        Renewal (ICCRS) 84

Continued......

11. A Journey in Faith - All Over the World 95

12. The International Charismatic Consultation
                        on World Evangelisation 115

13. Gatherings in the Holy Spirit 120

14. Charismatics and Pentecostals Together 124

15. Azusa Street - 100 Years of Blessing 132

16. CELEBRATE the Family 139

17. One For the Boys! 153

18. Called to Serve 158

19. Love One Another 168

20. All Things in Christ 179

21. There's Always More! 187

22. A Word from My Other Half 194

FOREWORD

I AM SO VERY GRATEFUL THAT OUR GOD IS A GOD OF SURPRISES! If this wasn't the case, no doubt Charles Whitehead would have spent his life as a loving family man and respected figure in the business world. But our God had even bigger plans for Charles. When you read this book you will see that Charles has been both a devoted father/grandfather and a very highly respected business man, but on top of all that he has been called, anointed, and sent into the Church as a powerful leader, tireless mentor, and gentle evangelist.

I am one of literally thousands of people who are spiritually indebted to Charles Whitehead. In 1986, as a fresh faced newly converted ex punk-rocker, I and several other young people stumbled into leading an explosive and very charismatic youth group in St. Albans called the Upper Room. Within a few months we were totally out of our depth as hundreds of often very needy young people began to meet with us every week to seek a touch of God the Father's awesome love. We needed help and God had just the person up His sleeve! Charles, and his amazing wife Sue, spent ten long years patiently sorting out our most dramatic messes.

My friendship, respect and need for Charles' wisdom didn't end there. As I got older, and the grey hairs of a young family man developed, I found myself working for Charles and the

Charismatic Renewal as an evangelist within the Church. With Charles' expert help we set up and have since been running CaFE (Catholic Faith Exploration) which has reached literally millions of people worldwide with the timeless message of Jesus through films, books, and parish missions.

During my thirty plus years of knowing, loving and learning from Charles, I have never ceased to be amazed at just how open he is to the leading of the Spirit. Many of us will spend our lives following the Lord in one way or another, but Charles has done this in countless ways; befriending Popes and normal church folk along the way. How he has managed to hold the many strands of his life together is a tribute to the power of the Holy Spirit (and a very strong wife!).

I hope you enjoy this wonderful journey and, like me, you will be left longing for the sequel *'Even More Surprises of the Spirit!'*

David Payne, 2020

INTRODUCTION

W HEN I LOOK BACK OVER MY LIFE, it is fascinating to see how the Holy Spirit has been at work since my earliest years, and to reflect on the parts played by a remarkable variety of people – Catholics, and Protestants, family and friends, clergy and religious, Popes and Pastors, the famous and the unknown. God's plan was full of the surprises of the Holy Spirit.

I have written this book because so many people have asked me to record the amazing things I have experienced in my life, believing that by doing so, many readers will find the encouragement needed to keep them going in their Christian walk when they are uncertain of the next steps. It is not really a book about the family life I have enjoyed with Sue and our children, but more about my personal spiritual journey.

I soon learned that I needed to keep moving in faith, trusting that the Lord would reveal His plans as I went forward. The very nature of our spiritual life is that it is in the hands of the Holy Spirit, and He will act in surprising and new ways when the time is right. Our part is to be always attentive to His leading, however surprising it may be, and to move ahead as He prompts us. Most of the book is about the things that have happened to me since I came to a living faith in 1976. But in the closing chapters, 18-21, I have tried to put all this into the context of God's plans for my spiritual formation and growth, and the lessons to be drawn from this will apply to most of us.

I hope you will find the following pages reassuring, written as they are by someone who has attempted to follow the leading of the Spirit even when it has seemed utterly amazing and way beyond what I was capable of doing. But today I am certain that with God all things are possible!

Charles Whitehead, 2020

CHAPTER ONE

THE STORY BEGINS

I WAS BORN ON OCTOBER 25TH 1942 DURING WORLD WAR II. My father was an officer in the British Army and was stationed in England while awaiting an overseas posting. He had enlisted and finished his training before war broke out – he had seen it coming and was finding his job boring – so he had been posted to France with the British Expeditionary Force but soon evacuated.

My place of birth is interesting, particularly as it is often requested when filling out official forms. I was born in Adlington Hall, Cheshire, one of our stately homes located near to Prestbury on the main road between Stockport and Macclesfield. It can be visited today as part of our national heritage but they have not yet installed the blue plaque with my name on it! It's interesting because it is almost all there is at Adlington and was a maternity home for officers' wives in the war years. My parents lived in the area before my father was posted abroad again early in 1943.

A YORKSHIRE FAMILY

The Whitehead family come from Yorkshire, although my father was born near Wimbledon when my grandfather was teaching at a school in London. They were Anglicans who attended church from time to time, some on a regular weekly basis. The family can be traced to Marsden, close to the

Yorkshire-Lancashire border, where my great-grandparents farmed up on the hills. At that time families were often large and our Whiteheads were no exception, numbering 12 children who survived childhood. Attending school involved a long daily walk across the moors and night-school was the same. In spite of this they were all well-educated with several entering the professions. My great-uncle Lewis, a librarian, wrote 'By-gone Marsden', a comprehensive history of the local area, and records of many Whitehead family members are to be found in the windows and on the tombstones at the local Anglican church, St. Bartholomews.

Two of the Whitehead brothers, Norman and Arthur, married two Wood sisters, Ida and Amy, resulting in more interaction than usual in our family relationships. While my grandfather Norman was a very successful head teacher, Arthur was an intelligent and sharp businessman, who established several successful companies, became a wealthy man and was looked upon as the head of the family. He lived south of Manchester, ultimately in Wilmslow, Cheshire, and had a holiday house by the sea in Prestatyn, North Wales, for the use of all the family, to which my grandparents retired when Norman stopped teaching.

THE CATHOLIC SIDE

My mother's side, the Hynes and Dean families, came originally from Galway in Ireland. Both families had come to England seeking a better life at a time of mass emigration from Ireland, and had settled in the Chorlton area south of

Manchester. My grandmother, Florence Dean, met and married Joseph Hynes, who like Norman Whitehead was also a teacher, holding a number of headships in Lancashire and Yorkshire during his professional life. After his retirement he established a small insurance business in Manchester which kept him occupied a couple of days a week. They retired to Gronant, a small village near to Prestatyn, for their closing years. For my mother's family, Prestatyn had always been their holiday choice and they had at times owned property there. Coming from Southern Ireland they were committed Catholics, always very involved in the life of the parish where they were living, and their faith played a key role in their lives.

A CATHOLIC-ANGLICAN WEDDING

My parents, Jack and Mary, had met in Prestatyn and were married in nearby Rhyl in January 1942. My father appreciated how important my mother's Catholic faith was to her, so they were married in the Catholic church, Our Lady of the Assumption, by a priest friend of her family, and my father happily agreed to bring up any children as Catholics. At that time the position of the Catholic Church was to accept a Catholic/Anglican marriage as long as it took place in a Catholic Church, but not to allow any music, flowers or a proper bridal wedding dress at the ceremony, as a sign that it was not a fully Catholic event. This did not deter my mother, and it just happened that the flowers for Sunday had been arranged early on the Saturday morning, the choir appeared to rehearse some wedding music just before the bride arrived, and her full length party dress happened to be white!

Talacre Abbey

Shortly after I was born, my father was posted abroad and he did not return until I was four years old, so my mother and I lived mainly with my maternal grandparents, part of the time in Gronant in the Prestatyn area. In Gronant there was an enclosed community of about 40 Benedictine nuns at Talacre Abbey, and my grandmother was very friendly with the Abbess, Mother Hilda. We regularly visited the Abbey for Mass and to see Mother Hilda, and were welcomed and looked after by two of the sisters who interfaced with the outside world, one of whom I remember was Sister Margaret Mary. These two were known as the *'outs'*. Mother Hilda used to talk to us through a small gap in a long screen which was veiled in black cotton material, because of course she was part of the enclosed community, the *'ins'*. One of my early memories is of my grandmother passing me through the screen so that Mother Hilda could hold and cuddle me. She would then take me to see the other enclosed sisters, who would also kiss and hug me and pass me from one to another. After this rather unusual experience (there were 40 Sisters!) Mother Hilda would take me into the chapel and sit me on the altar next to the tabernacle, before knocking on the door to tell Jesus that I had come to see him. She would then open the tabernacle door and bring out the Blessed Sacrament so that I could kiss Jesus. Of course all this was very naughty and against all the rules, but I really enjoyed it. I also received so much love and prayer from the sisters in this very special experience that it made a deep impression on me. I've liked nuns ever since!

A Surprising Visit

Many years later in 1996 I found myself in North Wales and decided to visit Prestatyn, Gronant, Talacre Abbey and the family graves in the nearby Franciscan friary of Pantasaph. When I came to the Abbey I went into the public chapel to pray, and happily remembered the many times I had been there as a young boy with my grandparents. As I was walking back to my car, an elderly nun appeared from the convent and came across to speak to me. She welcomed me and to my great surprise told me she knew who I was – Charles Whitehead, grandson of Florence and Joseph Hynes! I was amazed – my last visit to the Abbey had been in 1959 when I was about 17 years old. She asked me if I remembered who **she** was, and as I looked at her I realised she was Sister Margaret Mary – one of the two 'outs' I had known in my childhood! We had a wonderful conversation over a cup of tea, and she told me she had recognized me because she read GoodNews Magazine and often saw my photograph in it. Apparently when Pope St. John Paul II came to Liverpool, all the Talacre sisters had gone by coach to the big open-air Mass he celebrated, and she had bought a copy of the magazine from a young woman who was selling them there. When she found my photograph above an article I had written, she had taken out a subscription and maintained it ever since.

We spent a lot of time in North Wales in my early years, but when my father returned to civilian life and to his work in Manchester after the war, we settled in Wilmslow, and my brother Martin was born there in March 1947. We still visited

Prestatyn and Gronant regularly, as the area had a special place in the hearts of both my parents.

PREPARATION FOR FIRST COMMUNION

I remember that when I was about seven years old and preparing for my First Holy Communion in 1949, my classes in Wilmslow were interrupted as we spent our usual summer holidays in Prestatyn. So my grandmother arranged that the priest who was the chaplain to the nuns at Talacre Abbey and lived in a house adjacent to the convent, would continue my teaching while we were there. His name was Dom Hubert van Zeller, a Benedictine priest who was one of the foremost spiritual writers and directors of the time. His writings are still highly thought-of today. He had been sent to Talacre by his superiors to give him more time for his greatly sought-after writings, and he was happy to have the distraction of teaching a seven-year old first communicant. We used to go for walks in the woods and I remember how he talked to me about the love of Jesus, about his amazing teachings, the Cross, the Last Supper, our loving Father, and the exciting Holy Spirit. At the time I did not realise how blessed I was, but many of the things he said remained with me. Looking back now, I realise that even in those early days the Lord was preparing me for my future ministry, and Dom Hubert van Zeller was part of this.

LIFE WITH AUNTIE TESS

My grandparents' younger daughter, my Downs Syndrome Auntie Teresa always known as Tess, lived with them. She was a remarkable person and I learned an enormous amount from having her in my early life. She could never be left alone in the house because she totally trusted everyone and would have happily welcomed complete strangers and given them anything they wanted. At the same time, she liked to have her own way and to win any simple games we played – losing did not come easily to her! A most remarkable gift she had was to be able to play any piece of music she heard absolutely perfectly on a variety of musical instruments, without being able to read music and without ever having a single lesson on any of the instruments. She entertained us frequently on her piano accordion or sitting at the piano, playing and singing well-known hymns or current popular songs. She was a passionate supporter of Manchester United Football Club, and used to listen to radio commentaries on their matches (later watching them on television) wearing a bobble cap and swinging one of those old rattles that were popular years ago. She often stayed with us to give my grandparents a break, and when they were too old to care for her she lived permanently with us. I remember my father contacting Manchester United to ask if he could take her to see the Old Trafford ground one weekday, as she could never have coped with the crowds on a match day. They immediately invited him to take her on a normal Wednesday, and the then Manager, the famous Matt Busby, hosted them, entertained them for lunch, and showed her everything including all the trophies they had won. He had even arranged for her to go on the pitch to kick a ball around with Bobby Charlton, George Best and Denis Law, three of the most famous footballers in the world! From that day on, Matt Busby always sent Christmas and birthday cards to 'My Dearest Tess' signed 'Your friend Matt'. Tess used to go for holidays a couple of times a year to one of two convents where they cared for the sick, one in Bowden and the other in Manchester. She loved the convent life with its routines of prayer and daily Mass, and she helped the sisters by working in the kitchen, changing beds, and serving meals to the patients. The nuns were wonderful with her and I have occasionally met one who remembered her and spoke of her with huge affection. She died in 1980 and is greatly missed by all who knew her. Today there is great pressure to abort known Downs Syndrome babies, but my life would have been so much poorer without Tess, from whom I learned an amazing amount including what it means to receive unconditional love.

Pantasaph Friary

Another interesting thing about my maternal grandmother was that she was a Third Order Franciscan and we used to go regularly to Pantasaph Friary, about ten miles from where she lived in North Wales. In fact three generations of my family are buried there, including the ashes of both my parents. It's interesting to see the huge ornate tombstones marking the graves of my great-grandparents, which contrast with the modest stone marking where my grandparents and parents are at rest. My father died in 2015 at the age of ninety-nine and a half, and after the funeral in Sidmouth, Devon, where my parents had lived since his retirement in1985, we later took his ashes up to Pantasaph to join my mother who had died in 2000. I have always liked the small church at Pantasaph and was often taken there by my grandparents – it's one of those places with a very prayerful atmosphere and I remember praying there when I was quite young. I very much hope to continue going there from time to time to visit the family graves and to pray in the church – this will probably happen because my childhood memories have ensured that I like to visit North Wales. The local Charismatic Renewal has made good use of Pantasaph over the years, and been welcomed there for a variety of events.

A Roots Trip

In 2018 I took two of our boys, Adam and Tom, on a 'roots' trip over an August weekend, to visit North Wales, the parts of Cheshire around Wilmslow where I had grown up and our daughter Lucy had been born, to Stonyhurst College in Lancashire where Adam and I had both been to school, and then to Marsden in Yorkshire, the original home of the Whitehead family. Much of this was new to Adam and Tom, who had both been born in Buckinghamshire, where we had lived in the Chalfont St. Peter and Gerrards Cross area since the autumn of 1968. When we visited Pantasaph I took them into the small church, and as we were looking round it, a friar appeared and greeted us warmly. *'Hello, Charles, how nice to see you here. Are these two of your sons, visiting the family graves?'* The boys were amazed that he knew exactly who we were, but in fact he had attended our CELEBRATE Family Conference (see chapter 16). The trip was a great success and I hope to take our daughter Lucy and our other son Luke at some point in the future.

The whole trip with Adam and Tom was fascinating, but our visit to the Anglican church in Marsden was of particular interest. The graveyard was packed with Whiteheads, and St. Bartholomew's church itself had five stained glass windows presented by Whiteheads. A lady who was showing visitors around the church was delighted to meet us and promptly introduced us to two of her friends. Her father had bought his shop in Marsden from one of my great uncles, and she reminded us that Lewis Buckley Whitehead had been the town librarian and had written the fascinating book entitled *'By-gone Marsden'* mentioned earlier, a copy of which we had on our bookshelves at home.

I had a very happy and interesting childhood, the only sad part being the absence of my father in my early years, when he was serving overseas in the British army during World War II. Of course we prayed for him every night at my bed-time and kissed his photograph, but I remember that his much longed for return after the war was quite a shock – I was no longer the main focus of attention in the house, and while it was wonderful to have him back, it took a bit of getting used to for both of us!

CHAPTER TWO

THE FORMATIVE YEARS

EARLY SCHOOLDAYS

W HEN I WAS FIVE YEARS OLD we had settled in Wilmslow, and my schooldays began at Pownall Hall Preparatory School, just a few hundred yards from our house. It was a private Anglican school owned and run by the Clarke family and I enjoyed my time there. In chapter 19, when I write about ecumenism, I will describe my experience of being a Catholic boy in an Anglican school. My parents, particularly my mother, always wanted my brother and I to have a Public School education, and at quite a young age my name was put down for Stonyhurst College in Lancashire, the top Jesuit School in the country. So in September 1952, just before my tenth birthday, I started at St. Mary's Hall, the preparatory boarding school for Stonyhurst located just half a mile from the College. I remember having to take my food ration book with me as things were still not fully back to normal after the war. I settled in fairly quickly. We slept in dormitories of four and the daily time-table was strictly adhered to. As it was a Catholic school, the Jesuits followed a very strict programme of formation - each day started with Morning Prayer and Mass in the chapel and concluded with Night Prayer before bed. Every lesson started and finished with a prayer, we had Benediction at the weekends, said the Rosary regularly, went to weekly Confessions, had an occasional Retreat Day, and heard all about the particular Saint whose feast day we might be celebrating. There were about 150 boys there, and the staff included three Jesuit priests and a Scholastic in training to be a priest. The training to be a Jesuit priest is one of the longest of any religious order, lasting about fourteen years before final vows are taken. In true Jesuit tradition, physical punishment was an accepted part of the strict code of discipline. Sport was important in the life of the school – we played rugby in the winter and cricket in the summer, but tennis and athletics were also popular. My parents visited twice a term on Sundays and took me out for lunch and tea, otherwise writing a weekly letter home was a compulsory activity every Sunday morning after Mass. There were snooker and table tennis tables for recreation, and a film was often hired to be shown on a Saturday evening. Other memories include appearing in several plays, and learning a variety of poems for the termly elocution competitions, which I never won but received a commendation several times.

STONYHURST COLLEGE – HISTORY AND TRADITION

After three years at St. Mary's Hall I passed the entrance exam for Stonyhurst College itself and moved half a mile up the road to the very impressive College buildings in September 1955. The history of Stonyhurst as a Jesuit College is impressive; having spent some years in France during the time Catholicism was suffering persecution in England, returning when Parliament officially allowed Catholicism again and settling in the very impressive buildings at Stonyhurst which were gifted to the Jesuits by the **Weld** family.

UNIQUELY JESUIT

The names given to the classes at Stonyhurst are typically Jesuit and meaningless to most people – Rudiments, Figures, Grammar, Syntax, Poetry and Rhetoric. Furthermore the school was also divided up into 'Playrooms', which means that the whole of an academic year were kept together rather than being split up and allocated to different 'Houses' containing pupils of all ages – the norm in other similar Public Schools. For sport we were put into 'Lines', and I found myself in Weld, named after the Catholic family which had been such staunch supporters and benefactors of Stonyhurst. We slept in cubicles in quite large dormitories and a number of the staff were Jesuit priests at that time, taking care of supervision, discipline, and teaching responsibilities.

SIX CHALLENGING YEARS

I enjoyed my time at the College more than my three years at St. Mary's Hall, and entered into many of the wide range of activities on offer, some of which were compulsory whilst many were not. We had to join the Army Cadet Force, a very professional organisation headed up by a Colonel with a Regimental Sergeant Major, RSM Slack, the genuine article, who drilled us without let-up, resulting in Platoons and Companies of well-disciplined young men. I liked the Cadet Force and our summer camps at modern military bases, and I ended up as an Under-Officer responsible for a well-trained Company. I learned to shoot and even had a brief membership of the school Shooting Eight. I also enjoyed rugby as Captain of the School Third XV and an occasional member of the

Second XV. But my favourite game was tennis, at which I represented the school for several years and even had the excitement of competing in the Schools Wimbledon Tournament, playing on the Number Two court at Wimbledon club. Stonyhurst also had its own private golf course and I played there and at the Clitheroe Club. My Father was a keen golfer, his lowest handicap was three, and I had been helped with a special set of cut-down clubs and encouraged to play from the time my Father came home from World War Two. I never gave golf as much priority as he did, and my best years were at University when I played off a handicap of 12.

The College was very proud of its fine collection of antiques and paintings of all sorts, particularly its extensive array of liturgical and spiritual artefacts and relics, which attracted visitors from far and wide. So there was always much of interest to see and I am excited today that with the visionary leadership of our friend Lord Alton, the Christian Heritage Centre has been established in some converted buildings at Stonyhurst, which will attract visitors from all over the world. It offers good quality accommodation for individuals and groups in Theodore House and is well worth a visit.

FINAL WORDS OF WISDOM

Whilst hardly earth-shattering, my academic results were reasonably good, culminating in 'A' levels in History, English and French and a place at Durham University. In my last few days at the College, the Rector gave a special talk to the leavers. The part that has stayed with me is when he told us that if we were guests in someone else's home, we must always be sure to compliment the chef and to make sure the bath was clean after we used it. I cannot imagine such words of wisdom are still shared today!

AN ACADEMIC SPIRITUALITY

My spiritual life was fairly active, not really from personal choice but because it was a vital part of the curriculum we followed. We were in chapel three times a day including morning Mass, prayer was a regular part of each day, and we had a three day Retreat at the start of each academic year. I took all this very much for granted, but the school holidays always found me at Sunday Mass with my family. I won the class prize for Religious Education several times over the years, and built up a very good understanding of Catholic doctrine and teaching. Looking back I can clearly see that this was all very academic, but at the time it was what was expected. The Jesuits never really spoke to us about their own faith or their call to the priesthood in a personal way, although I knew they were very holy men and that their faith and priesthood were the most important things in their lives. The thought of becoming a priest never really entered my head – I was more interested in girl-friends and felt sure I would get married and have a family. But my faith was genuine, if rather mechanical and intellectual and not really alive.

TWO LIFE-CHANGING YEARS

In my penultimate year at the College, an elderly chain-smoking Jesuit priest had recognised leadership potential in me and had appointed me joint head of my year and senior monitor in my dormitory. He clearly saw something others had not seen (with the exception of the Cadet Force Colonel) and he invested quite a bit of time in talking to me and encouraging me. The fruit of this was that in my final year I was a member of the School Committee of ten, who were the hand-picked top boys, with responsibility for leadership and discipline in every area of the lives of the boys of all ages. We had the power to issue detention notices, to withdraw privileges, and at that time even to deliver corporal punishment when all ten of us were of one mind. In return for accepting such responsibilities, we enjoyed a number of privileges which included having one of the finest top-floor individual private bed-sitting rooms overlooking the half-mile drive up to the College, known as The Avenue, which runs between two artificial lakes, occupied by ducks, geese and swans. When I look back, I realise how much I learned in my last two years at Stonyhurst, and what a lot I owe to my elderly, slightly eccentric mentor, Fr. Bill Corbishley.

AMAZING FAITH

My younger brother, Martin, was also educated at Stonyhurst, and went on to become a chartered accountant. During his time at the College he suffered a very serious illness and spent some weeks in hospital in Preston and then at the Manchester Royal Infirmary. There were times when my parents were told that he might not live, and it was my mother's amazing faith that kept them going, as she prayed and interceded at his bedside and in the hospital chapels. He made a full recovery, and my mother's faith had so moved my father that he joined the Catholic Church, where he was a very faithful, committed and active member for the rest of his life. Martin married Pat who came from Australia. They have two children, Alice and Toby, three grandchildren, and live near Lyme Regis on the Devon-Dorset border, where he is in private practice as an accountant and financial advisor.

KEEPING IN TOUCH

I have tried to maintain my links with Stonyhurst, and in the 1990s I was invited back to speak to the students about their faith on several occasions. I served for two years as the President of the Old Boys Association, for five years as a School Governor, and I'm impressed with the solid, all-round education the College still offers. In 2019 I was invited to speak at the Easter Retreat for alumni and parents, at which columnist Francis Davis was one of the participants and speakers, and in his article in the Catholic Times after the event he said he was *'impressed and inspired'* by what I said. That's always good to hear!

THE CALL TO HIGHER EDUCATION

In my last year at Stonyhurst I faced the challenge of what to do next, but that was an easy decision – I had always wanted to go to university. I was advised to apply to Cambridge to read history, and invited to sit entrance exams for Gonville and Caius College. After the exams I was invited for a further interview but was not offered a place. Part of the reason was probably the fact that my interviewer had spent the previous summer vacation at Stonyhurst College working on a new book, and so knew every single historical tome in the school library. Sadly the fact that I did not share this knowledge, and had read very few of them anyway, had obviously not impressed him!

DURHAM UNIVERSITY

So I applied to Durham University and to Trinity College, Dublin, receiving acknowledgements from both and an invitation to choose a Durham College and to attend for interview. Much to my delight my best friend at home, James McCarter, was also applying to Durham, although for totally different subjects, so we went up for our interviews together. We both immediately loved Durham, were accepted for our subjects, applied to and became members of the same College, **St. Cuthbert's Society.** First year students, 'Freshers', did not live in College, so we found digs in a shared room at the home of Mrs. Wilson on The Avenue. What happened to Trinity College, Dublin? Well, I received an offer of a place during my first week in residence in Durham for the Freshers Conference - better late than never, I suppose! So late September 1961 found me at Durham University studying for a General Arts Degree in History, English and French. My primary subject was history and I had opted to study American History on the rather unedifying grounds that it was going to be a lot shorter and less complicated than European History. In fact I only had four lectures a week, which left me with plenty of time for other things – particularly snooker, bridge, and a very active social life. We didn't survive much more than the first term in

Mrs. Wilson's comfortable digs on The Avenue. She was a nice, maternal Geordie widow who treated us well and cooked extremely fine breakfasts. The problem was that my friend Jim could not resist testing some disused gas lights on the walls in our bedroom. They worked brilliantly but as there were no mantles they scorched a large area of the ceiling. Our offer to re-paint the ceiling was accepted but once the job was done we were politely asked to leave. Jim went into a flat, sharing with two people, and I found a nice room a short distance from Durham Market Place.

A NEW FREEDOM
I found life in Durham exhilarating and liberating. After the understandable discipline and constraints of a Public School and the limitations inherent in holidays at home, it was amazing to be totally free to do whatever I wanted.

In my first year I mainly went out with local girls. The thinking behind this was simple – local knowledge, home-cooked meals, the possibility of borrowing a family car, local parties. My girl-friend from the second term of my first year was **Janice** – a very popular 18 year old Geordie girl whose father happened to be the landlord of one of the most frequented student pubs, the Buffalo's Head, located on The Bailey, the road that went down to several Colleges including St. Cuthberts. Their family car was a large Standard Vanguard and her dad was happy to lend us this for trips out. In return I helped at busy times in the bar and Janice's mother provided home-cooked meals. Janice was great and through her I got to know quite a lot of local people, including Joe, a widower and retired Geordie coal miner, who took me and my friend Ian Philip in as lodgers in our second year. Joe had spent a few years in the Army Catering Corps and was an excellent cook, our only problem was that he was broad Geordie, pretty unintelligible to a lad like me from Cheshire and to Ian, a Yorkshireman. But he was a lovely man and we got on famously, often drinking together in the pub near our digs. He had a friendly dog, Jacko, a Jack Russell terrier, who came everywhere with Joe, always to the pub where he had his own special doggie bowl behind the bar so he could have a beer with us. I remember the first time I went to the pub with Joe and Jacko, I was buying the second round, so I was ordering a second half pint for Jacko when Joe stopped me: *'Why man, yer canna do that! He'll be p----d and you'll have to carry him hem!'* At the end of my first year Janice and I decided to call it a day and parted as good friends. I like the Geordies – they are a very genuine and straightforward people.

During my time at Durham I went to church only occasionally. I was always expected to be able to answer questions about Christianity, raised over a few beers in pubs, and frankly I was well able to do this thanks to the Jesuits, even though the practice of my faith left much to be desired. I never lost my faith, but a lot of other things took priority over the expression of it, even in a wonderfully Christian city like Durham with its amazing history and beautiful Cathedral. I used to telephone home every Sunday lunchtime, and my mother would always ask me if I had been to church. So I established a habit of going into the back of the local Catholic Church of St. Cuthbert, making the sign of the cross with holy water, genuflecting, and coming straight out again to go into the red telephone box outside. When asked the usual question, I could truthfully reply *'I've just come out of church'*, but I doubt that this fooled my mother.

THREE

A Perfect Partner

My time in Durham fell into two parts – from September 1961 up to May 1963, and from then until I graduated and left in June 1965. Why the division? Because in May 1963 I met **Sue Watkins**, a first year science student from St. Aidan's College who came from Cardiff, and my life was wonderfully changed. As I went around Durham City I had noticed this dark-haired, smiling, attractive girl from St. Aidan's College, but I had no idea who she was. One evening a friend of mine was giving a fancy-dress party and he had asked me to take charge of whatever drinks people brought with them. So I was stationed at the entrance in my Doc Halliday fancy dress, a boot-lace tie and a pistol, relieving everyone of their drinks and either pouring them into the large bowl of 'punch' or adding their bottles to the drinks table. The dark-haired attractive girl from St. Aidans College arrived unaccompanied, dressed in a black slip and high heels, as 'I Want To Be Evil', the title of a current Eartha Kitt hit song. She knew no-one at the party except the host, so we started chatting and I quickly passed over my door-keeping responsibilities to a friend so that Sue – that was her name – and I could talk and dance together all evening. At the end of the evening I took her back to her College, invited her out on a date the next evening, and she accepted!

FALLING IN LOVE
I was fortunate to have an old Mini Traveller in my second year at Durham, so the next evening I drove us out to Blanchland, about 15 miles west of Durham across beautiful open moorland countryside and the site of an old monastery with a great country hotel, The Lord Crewe Arms, where we enjoyed a drink and a snack. When I dropped Sue back at her College I told her I had fallen in love with her and after our next date I told her I thought we would get married after university! My friends thought I was mad - I should play it cool and let things take their course, but I was certain she was the one for me and of course we got engaged in July 1965 after finishing at Durham and were married on September 10th 1966.

We thoroughly enjoyed one another's company during the rest of that summer term, but unfortunately Sue failed her first year exams and had to return for re-sits during the summer vacation. I must make it clear that her failing had little to do with me – she had done hardly any work all year, thoroughly enjoying representing the University at hockey, being a member of the Athletic Union, and taking an active part in organising social events for the University.

UNCONDITIONAL LOVe
A moment I have never forgotten came when Sue telephoned home to say she had failed. She reversed the charges, using one of the traditional red telephone boxes, and her father answered. I couldn't hear their conversation but after a couple

of minutes she opened the door of the box, held out the telephone to me and said, *'He wants to speak to you!'* Nervously I took the phone - *'Hello, Mr. Watkins'*, fearing he might say *'Get out of my daughter's life – you're obviously a bad influence'*, but no. *'Hello, Charles, I'm looking forward to seeing you here in Cardiff during the holidays. I'd like you to do something for me. Take Susan out for dinner; go to the most expensive restaurant in Durham, probably at The Royal County Hotel, and buy yourselves the most expensive dinner on the menu. Have a bottle of champagne, pay the bill and send it to me. I'll refund you by return.'* *'Sue did tell you she failed'* I stuttered. *'Yes, she did and that's a pity, but the important thing right now is that she knows she is loved for who she is and not for what she does'*. This taught me an amazing lesson I have never forgotten, because this is exactly how our Heavenly Father would react. This was a living, human example of God's unconditional love for each one of us. As I travel the world, speaking at Christian Conferences and events, I've told the story many times to incredible effect. People gasp, some burst into tears – but please God all learn a lesson they never forget. Sue has never had any problem knowing how much God loves her, after all, she had a living example of this in her own father. She passed her re-sits and we continued our committed relationship at Durham University until we left in July 1965. But our remaining time there was not without complications, caused by some unexpected problems with my health.

A MONTH IN CANNES
At the end of term in July 1963 I went to Cannes in France to

follow an international 4 week long language course designed to improve my spoken French. It was a very enjoyable course, we only worked mornings, and Cannes in July-August was an amazing place to be. But there was a problem. I was part of the English-speaking group with a mix of Americans, Canadians, Australians, Japanese, Chinese, Scandinavians - in fact anyone from anywhere in the world who could speak English more than French! The inevitable result was that we all spoke English in our free time rather than French, and this was not the aim of the course. But Cannes was an enjoyable experience.

GOD SAVE THE QUEEN!

I became good friends with a young American called Peter, who rented an Austin Healey sports car in which we drove around the town and along the coast. I remember a particular evening hosted by the Lord Mayor of Cannes, when every nation was asked to perform their national song or dance. We saw some wonderful examples from different countries with everyone in national dress which they had brought with them, but the only thing the UK group could come up with was 'God Save the Queen', sung standing formally to attention and saluting! I came home after an enjoyable five weeks, but much improvement in my French was hard to detect. Sue and I resumed our very happy relationship and we returned to Durham at the end of September for what should have been my final year.

21ST BIRTHDAYS

At the end of a very good autumn term which included my

21st birthday, we spent Christmas with our respective families and in January I went down to Cardiff to celebrate Sue's 21st birthday on the 10th with a party for all her family and friends. When I returned home I was beginning to feel unwell, and after my doctor had referred me to a chest specialist, I was diagnosed with pleural tuberculosis and sent to Manchester Royal Infirmary for further tests and a more detailed diagnosis. I ended up in Baguley Infirmary, just south of Manchester, where I spent two months having daily injections and special treatment. The man responsible for me was junior Doctor Pain – not the greatest surname for a medical practitioner! When I was discharged I went home to my parents on a daily dose of some very large special tablets which I took for two years. Having lost a whole term, I did not return to Durham that academic year, but went back in the September to do a full final year. Throughout my illness, Sue visited and spent time with me as often as she could. Her commitment and faithfulness were quite remarkable and convinced me – if that was even necessary – that I was absolutely right in my decision that she was the one with whom I wanted to spend the rest of my life. A couple of minutes ago, 56 years later, she has just appeared to sort out a problem I am having with my computer as I type this!

OUR FINAL YEAR
Returning to Durham in September 1964, I resumed my course in its final year and had the opportunity to spend much of my time with Sue who was then also in her final year. She was living in the newly built St. Aidan's College just across the

river from the city, and I was in St. Cuthbert's accommodation nearer the centre. We both thoroughly enjoyed our final year, in which Sue captained the ladies hockey team, played for Durham county, and in her capacity as Vice-President of the University Athletics Union she organised most of the University's social events. The new University Sports Centre near Shincliffe was opened during the year by the captain of the Welsh national rugby team, and Sue's name appears on the special plaque commemorating the event. For my part, I played bridge and snooker for my College, some tennis and golf, and graduated with a second class degree. Sue in fact failed her finals, but when it came to finding a job was much in demand by the newly established computer industry which recognised her inherent abilities as a programme writer, resulting in well-paid job offers from IBM, ICT and Honeywell. She chose to join ICT as a programmer in their local government sector, working in Newcastle, Leeds, Manchester and Liverpool, at a higher salary than I was able to command!

SWEDISH EMPLOYERS

I was offered jobs after interview by two or three commercial companies, but took the decision to join the Whitehead Paper Agency, a family company working mainly with the Swedish Paper Industry. I did this because my experience of holiday jobs in Sweden, and the enthusiasm of the Swedes in encouraging me to work for them after university, had led me to believe that this industry offered me excellent career opportunities. And so it proved to be. After I had worked for almost three years in the Whitehead Paper Agency in

Manchester, the company was bought by a large Swedish paper group, Fiskeby Aktiebolag, and I was transferred to London as Sales Manager for their new UK company in 1968.

I stayed with this Swedish Group through a number of take-overs until my retirement in the year 2000 at the age of 58, serving as Managing Director of a number of UK subsidiary companies over the years and Chairman of their UK Group. During my working life I also served as President of the UK Paper Agents Association, I was a founder member and Chairman of the Institute of Paper, was invited to join the Stationers and Paper Makers Livery Company, became a Freeman of the City of London, and a Fellow of the Institute of Directors. I thoroughly enjoyed my years in industry and my relationship with the Swedish companies, and in a later chapter I will explain how I came to work only half-time but on a full salary for over ten years. Today, 20 years since my retirement, I still go to an annual meeting with about 12 of my old paper industry staff, for a very happy and enjoyable lunch and afternoon together on the banks of the river Thames, near the Tower of London.

ENGAGED AND MARRIED
Following my graduation, Sue and I got engaged just after leaving Durham in 1965, with the wedding set for September 1966 at St. Brigid's Catholic Church in Sue's parish of Cyncoed in Cardiff. Sue had been brought up in the Anglican Church (Church of Wales), but with all the wisdom of a 17 year old science student had decided that God did not exist, so had

become an atheist. Although my church-going was somewhat irregular, my Catholic faith was important to me, and Sue recognised this. So on September 10th 1966 we were married in Cardiff by a Jesuit priest friend, Fr. Ben Winterborn, College Principal at Campion Hall, Oxford University, assisted by Sue's Anglican uncle, Reverend Haydn Humphries, the Vicar of Dewsbury in Yorkshire, and we settled in our first home, a two-bedroomed semi-detached cottage in Bramhall, Cheshire, for which we paid £2,100!

Our wedding day 10th September 1966
at St. Brigid's Church, Cardiff

Our daughter, **Lucy**, was born in nearby Altrincham in March 1968, and in September that year my Swedish employers opened their London office on Tower Hill, and I was transferred there. So in the November we moved down to

Chalfont St. Peter, Buckinghamshire, to a three-bedroomed semi-detached house within commuting distance of London for which we paid £7,000. We had initially looked at houses to the south of London but chose Chalfont St. Peter on the north west side because we loved the area; it was quite close to Heathrow Airport for my trips to Sweden, and when I travelled around the UK for my work I went mostly to the north and west of London.

Our second child, **Adam**, was born in March 1969, but it was ten years later before our third child, **Luke**, was born, followed by number four, **Tom**. With the four children we moved to a large family house, which we named *'The Open House'* in nearby Gerrards Cross in 1978, but when they had all left home 28 years later we moved back to Chalfont St. Peter, and since 2006 we have lived in a three-bedroomed detached house, *'Holly Trees'*, which we love and is very close to St. Joseph's Catholic Church, Gold Hill Baptist Church, and the Village Centre, very suitable for an older couple.

FOUR

LIFE-CHANGING MOMENTS

IN 1974 WE MOVED HOUSE WITHIN CHALFONT ST. PETER and became very friendly with Janet and Colin Hession and their two children who lived opposite us. They were very committed Anglicans, and in 1976 they invited us to join an ecumenical discussion group they were hosting in their home to talk about their Christian faith. The group consisted of Anglicans, Baptists and Catholics, and they thought that my atheist wife, Sue, would stimulate some interesting discussions! I did not find the first meeting very helpful as everyone seemed entrenched in their views, but my dear wife thoroughly enjoyed the disagreements and lack of unity. Our second meeting was very different, because a Baptist couple, Jim and Ina Hamilton, shared their faith in Jesus Christ in a very personal way, telling us how they were aware of the Holy Spirit guiding them in everything. This provoked a fascinating discussion, and when we got home we talked at length about the impact this had made.

WAS THERE REALLY A GOD AFTER ALL?
Having noticed the effect they had on Sue, Ina popped in the next day with a modern translation of the Bible as a gift for her – we had been using her old family Bible, the King James translation. Ina suggested she might like to read the New Testament letters, and as she did this, Sue found them both real and interesting. A week or two later, I went up to

Aberdeen on a business trip and Sue saw an interview on TV with Margaret Court, the Australian Wimbledon tennis champion, who at the time was a Catholic. Margaret talked about her faith in just the same way as Jim and Ina had done, and Sue was fascinated that here was a Catholic expressing exactly the same views as our Baptist friends. Was there really a God after all, because if so, not to believe in him would mean she was on the wrong side! So when she went to bed, Sue prayed and asked God to reveal himself if he really was there. She had tried but failed to generate faith herself – he had to do something. As she said this she was overcome with light and heat – as if a pilot light had been turned on deep inside her and was gradually increasing until her whole body seemed to be on fire. Her response was to promise to keep that fire burning, and she fell asleep. On waking up the next morning she knew that her heavenly Father had created her, that Jesus had died for her, that the Spirit was alive in her, and she responded in thanksgiving and praise! Life was going to be different.

A LIFE-CHANGING CHALLENGE

The next day I came home from Aberdeen to be met by Lucy and Adam with the exciting news that, *'Mum's got God! And she's nicer than she was yesterday!'* This presented me with a major challenge – I now had a wife with a living faith, alive in the Spirit, whereas my faith remained purely intellectual. Some weeks later, we went as a family one Sunday morning to a nearby Anglican church, St. Andrews, Chorleywood, because Sue had heard that the Holy Spirit was moving there.

We arrived just as the service was about to start and were shown to the only empty seats – in the front row! We very much enjoyed the service which was lively, suitable for the children and with an excellent sermon on Jesus meeting the Samaritan woman at the well (John chapter 4). So as we were leaving, I shook his hand and thanked the curate, Rev. Barry Kissell, for his excellent sermon. He made no response but stared into my eyes. Thinking he was trying to remember if he knew me, I continued to make small talk but without any response until he suddenly said, '*Do you know how much God loves you? I'd like to pray with you*'. He took me back into the church and spent a few minutes praying for me. When he prayed in a strange language I thought he must be a foreigner – I had never heard anyone praying in tongues, which is what he was doing. After a time of silence he invited me for coffee in the Church Hall, collecting Sue and the children on the way. He declined to answer my questions, simply saying that God would make everything clear, which I found very frustrating.

'PRAISE MY SOUL THE KING OF HEAVEN!'
The next morning I went to work as usual, and at that time my office was in the City of London. As my mind was full of questions about what God was doing, I found it hard to concentrate and so I went out for a walk mid- morning, finding my way into St. Mary Moorfields, a small Catholic church not far from my office. As I knelt at the front before the tabernacle, I was suddenly overwhelmed with a sense of God's presence and his love for me personally. I found myself repenting of things that were wrong in my life, lying on the floor and

praying in a strange language, standing up and praising God aloud in hymns I remembered from my childhood, and just enjoying the amazing experience of God's love for me. When I eventually looked at my watch, I realised I had been there for a very long time and hurried back to my office. As I went up Moorgate, I noticed people were stepping aside to let me pass, even stepping off the pavement. How strange, I thought, but suddenly realised I was singing *'Praise my soul, the King of Heaven!'* at the top of my voice – not a very common occurrence in the City of London at lunchtime!

'I'VE BEEN EXPECTING YOU TO CALL!'

Arriving home that evening, I excitedly told Sue what had happened and telephoned Rev. Barry Kissell. *'I've been expecting you to call,'* he said, *'come on over'*. When I arrived he greeted me warmly and explained that he was learning to listen to the promptings of the Holy Spirit, and then to say what he felt he was hearing. So I told him my experience that morning and he simply said, *'God is transforming your life – He has great things for you to do'*. No-one has ever spoken truer words to me. He prayed for me and I went home, wondering what all this could mean. I knew nothing about the Charismatic Renewal (explained in chapter 6) at this time, but gathered that I had experienced baptism in the Holy Spirit, which had promptly brought my very intellectual faith alive in a most remarkable way.

AMAZING LOVE

Today I know that without this all-embracing influence of

God's love deep within us, we will struggle to love and accept ourselves, to totally trust the prompting and guidance of the Spirit, to love and accept others unconditionally, and to be willing to step out in faith no matter what our human logic may be saying to us. If these doubts remain with us, we are very likely to fail to achieve God's purposes for our lives. In contrast, being utterly convinced of God's amazing love for us makes it so much easier to share His love with others and to receive love from them. But to come to this point is often a process – it does not happen all at once.

I was a product of one of the very best Catholic educations money could buy, and my intellectual understanding of my faith was at a very high level. I was living life in accordance with good Christian values, but without realising that I needed to surrender totally to the Person of the Holy Spirit. Only if this happened would I really become the person I was created to be, and to bring this about God chose to use a number of people who were already following the promptings of His Spirit on a daily basis, which they immediately did again in my case with amazing results.

FIVE

Praying Friends

WHEN SUE AND I WERE BAPTISED IN THE HOLY SPIRIT in 1976, we were invited to join a local ecumenical prayer group which met weekly at the Convent of the Holy Cross Sisters in Chalfont St. Peter in our parish. Two of the sisters led the group which numbered about 25 regular attenders, made up of local Anglican, Baptist and Catholic Christians, with the Catholics in the majority. Within a couple of years we were members of the small leadership team, and soon after this, changes in the sisters' community meant that the group needed to find a new meeting place and ended up in our home. We later moved to the larger family house in Gerrards Cross which we re-named *'The Open House'*, and naturally the Prayer Group came with us and stayed for 26 years until we downsized and moved back to Chalfont St. Peter in 2006.

FRIDAY EVENINGS

The Holy Cross Prayer Group, as it was known, was certainly one of the greatest influences in my life. The weekly Friday evening meeting was open to all and we enjoyed the presence of a wide variety of people of all ages and backgrounds. When Sue and I were away from home, one of the leaders had a key to 'The Open House' and the group met there in our absence. It was always ecumenical and we were blessed by visits from a variety of Charismatic Renewal and Church leaders over the years. We organised Life in the Spirit Seminars from time to time, and week after week the members of the group exercised their charismatic gifts of prophecy, speaking in tongues, healing, words of knowledge, etc in our meetings. We never had a formal music ministry, but enjoyed very free and open praise and worship, with members starting and leading us in hymns and choruses as the Spirit inspired them. The numbers fluctuated week by week between about 20 and 30, and we built up strong, close and long-lasting relationships of love and trust over the years. The Holy Spirit moved powerfully among us and it would be impossible to list the countless occasions when people's lives were touched and changed.

Every meeting ended with tea and biscuits, during which people mingled and chatted, and private prayer ministry was always available in an adjoining room. We celebrated the main feasts in the church's year, we had visiting speakers on a regular basis, and enjoyed an annual summer barbecue and a Christmas party. Outside the prayer meetings, those who needed help and care of any sort were looked after, and special occasions in people's lives were appropriately celebrated.

DAILY PRAYER SUPPORT

Of course there were times when I was returning home on a Friday evening after a hectic week or a trip abroad, just wanting a quiet evening, but within minutes of joining the Prayer Group I was blessed by the praise and worship, encouraged by the teaching, and overwhelmed by the peace and joy of the Holy Spirit. I know too that whatever I was doing and wherever I was going, I had the daily prayer support of members of the group who had committed themselves to praying for us. One of the very faithful members of the group was an elderly lady called Bessie. She carried a photograph in her handbag of us both and prayed for us regularly. One Friday evening, I asked for prayer because I had received an invitation to lead a Healing Service at St. Albans Anglican Abbey. *'I hope you said 'no' – it's not your ministry'*, was Bessie's immediate response. When I asked why she thought this, her reply was *'Whenever you pray for my healing I always get worse!'* Now I could accept what she said because I knew how much she loved me and prayed for me, and to be honest, she was right - healing is not really my ministry. I declined the invitation.

AMAZING FRUIT
Over the years we were blessed by some amazing praise and worship, by excellent teaching, anointed prayer ministry, but probably above all by the sense that the Lord was very present and speaking to us in a whole variety of ways, often through shared Scriptures, all under the inspiration of the Holy Spirit. The charismatic dimension was strong as were the quiet times of devotion and reflection, the moving occasions of personal sharing, and of course the prayer needs so often met by the Lord.

Probably the most extensive early fruit of the Charismatic Renewal was the emergence and growth of so many different kinds of prayer groups, meeting in people's homes, in parish halls, convents, schools and public buildings. In my personal experience of 30 years of our prayer group, I fully understood the appeal and the blessing of a good charismatic prayer group, and my only regret is that even more were not established and that currently there is a decline in their numbers in some countries, including our own. Young people today have not been drawn to these old-style groups as we were, but have their own ways of meeting for worship, teaching and fellowship.

BAPTISM IN THE HOLY SPIRIT – THE HEART OF IT ALL

Many people still think of the Catholic Charismatic Renewal as a prayer group movement, but this is to misunderstand and to limit what it really is. The heart of this Renewal has always been baptism in the Holy Spirit, a life-changing personal experience of the release and out-pouring of the Holy Spirit in the life of an individual, the fruit of which is a transformed spiritual life and the desire to express and live this in a whole variety of ways – just one of which is by gathering for prayer, praise, worship, and ministry with others who share the same life-changing experience. So prayer groups are a vibrant and dynamic expression of this, but it is also expressed in a whole range of other ways too. For me, our Holy Cross Prayer Group was an essential part of my spiritual growth, providing a consistent and reliable way of encountering the Lord every week in the midst of my exciting but very challenging and diverse spiritual journey. This journey took me into significant areas of leadership responsibility – locally, nationally and internationally. I remain eternally grateful for the stability and

refreshment our praying friends brought into my life every
Friday evening.

SPIRITUAL GIFTS OR CHARISMS

I quickly learned that accepting baptism in the Holy Spirit
doesn't mean joining a movement. It means embracing the
fullness of my Christian initiation. It can touch anyone and
everyone. It has an effect on every part of the life of the Church
because it equips us to serve God and one another in love and
power, and sends us out to participate in the Church's mission
to the world. It can revitalise every programme and activity in
my parish because it can revitalise every person involved in
those programmes and activities. Living my life in the Spirit
means participating fully in the body of Christ. It can help to
make my parish a real community of love from which I
take the challenge of the Gospel into my social and work
environments. My mission is to transform society, and the
presence and the power of the Holy Spirit is essential if this is
to happen. At a public audience in 1992, Pope St. John Paul II
taught on the charisms in the life of the Church. He explained
their importance in these words: *'The People of God's sharing in
the Messianic Mission is not obtained only through the Church's
ministerial structure and sacramental life. It also occurs in other
ways – that of the spiritual gifts or charisms'* (L'Osservatore
Romano, no. 26, 1st July 1992).

A GRACE FOR US ALL

If I am to play a full part in the mission of the Church, I need
the charismatic gifts of the Holy Spirit. They come to me

through baptism in the Holy Spirit, a grace God freely offers to everyone. But it's a grace that must be desired, requested, appropriated and put into practice - that is the challenge of the Charismatic Renewal. May I continue to respond to it myself and to be always looking for new ways of helping others to do so.

SIX

A GRACE FOR US ALL

CHARISMATIC RENEWAL

AFTER MY TIME WITH THE ANGLICAN CURATE and my experience in St. Mary Moorfield Church in the City of London, I found that I could pray in tongues. *'Oh! You're a Charismatic now!'* someone told me. Many people have heard something about the Catholic Charismatic Renewal (CCR) without really understanding it, which is a pity, because Charismatic Renewal is a gift from God and has something extremely important to bring into the life of the Church. So against this background I will try to summarise in a short and easily understandable way what lies at the heart of the CCR and why it is so important for the life of the Church. I'll begin by looking at the two words *'charismatic'* and *'renewal'* as used in this context.

CHARISMS

A charism is a special gift of the Holy Spirit. It has its root in the Greek word 'charis' meaning 'grace'. Every charism is a special gift of grace because it is supernaturally given by the Holy Spirit to equip the recipient to undertake a particular task or service for the benefit and up-building of the Church. So the word *'charismatic'* is used here to describe something that has its origins in, is inspired by, and contains the power of, the Holy Spirit. The word *'charismatic'* is a descriptive adjective and should never be used as a noun.

RENEWAL

The Oxford English Dictionary defines *'renewal'* in these words: *'among charismatic Christians, the state or process of being renewed in the Holy Spirit'*. So *'renewal'* is a process usually beginning when the Holy Spirit responds to a request to renew someone's spiritual life. Every Christian needs on-going spiritual renewal, and here we are clearly reminded by the Oxford Dictionary that this is an activity of the Holy Spirit. In fact, Pope Francis has explained the Charismatic Renewal in these words: *'You, the Charismatic Renewal, have received a great gift from the Lord. Your movement's birth was willed by the Holy Spirit to be 'a current of grace in the Church and for the Church'. This is your identity: to be a current of grace'* *(Rome, June 1st 2014)*.

Drawing all this together and keeping it simple, we can say that the CCR is in essence both the action and the result of an outpouring of the Holy Spirit which brings a new or renewed experience of God's life and power into the lives of His individual children. It is a sovereign work of the Holy Spirit of God because it is not something we own or control. Through it we are invited to hand our lives over to God and to give the control to Him. We allow God to **BE** God and to work in and through us by His Holy Spirit to equip and empower us to live effective Christian lives. This renewal is freely available to anyone who asks – we just need to be willing to invite the Holy Spirit to release His power in us and to bring alive the graces of our baptism. But the Spirit not only brings alive all that we have already received through the sacraments of our Christian initiation – He also comes to us again in power to equip us with new gifts or charisms for service and mission.

A MOVE OF THE SPIRIT

The CCR is not a single, unified worldwide movement; it does not have a human founder or formal programme of initiation and membership lists as other movements do. Neither is it a special devotion to the Holy Spirit, a new spirituality for some particular people, or just a network of prayer groups and communities. In 1990 Cardinal Leon Josef Suenens explained it in these words:

> *'To interpret the Renewal as a movement among other move-*
> *ments is to misunderstand its nature; it is a movement of the*
> *Spirit offered to the entire Church, and destined to rejuvenate*
> *every facet of the Church's life. The soul of Renewal, Baptism*
> *in the Spirit, is a grace of Pentecostal refreshment offered to*
> *all Christians.'*

ENORMOUS VARIETY

The Charismatic Renewal is a highly diverse collection of individuals, groups, communities, ministries and activities, usually independent of each other, in different stages and modes of development and with different emphases. One of the special characteristics of the CCR is the enormous variety of expressions and ministries, all inspired by the Holy Spirit and carried out in His power, which have a home under the CCR umbrella. Everyone shares the same simple foundational experience of the empowering presence of the Holy Spirit

through baptism in the Spirit, but the emphasis is on
relationships and networks rather than on structures and
organisation. These patterns of informal relationships are to
be found at local, diocesan, national and international levels
and are characterised by free association, dialogue and
collaboration. Many groups feel they are part of a big
charismatic family, and by their very nature are related to
each other. They know they are fully part of the Church under
the hierarchy, and that is important to them. The simple desire
of those involved is that as many others as possible should also
have their Christian lives renewed by the Holy Spirit. Some
organisation may be necessary to facilitate this but it should
be kept simple. The CCR is a current of grace in the great river
of the Church, bringing the power of Pentecost into every part
of her life and mission, offering a fuller life in the Spirit to
everyone. It is this fuller life into which I had unknowingly
entered in 1976, and which was to prove totally life-changing.

CHARIS - A Sign of God's Blessing

As I was finishing this book, something extremely important
happened in Rome at Pentecost 2019. A remarkable new phase
in the life of the Catholic Charismatic Renewal known as
CHARIS was officially launched by Pope Francis. He had
introduced the concept of CHARIS about three years earlier
when he asked Michelle Moran, a Past President of ICCRS
(International Catholic Charismatic Renewal Services), and
Pino Scafuro, a Vice President of the Catholic Fraternity of
Covenant Communities, to draft one new official document
to cover all the many worldwide expressions of the Catholic

Charismatic Renewal. The Pope's vision was to have one single organisation to serve and promote the whole CCR rather than a number of different bodies, each with their own private Statutes and structures, covering particular expressions of the Renewal. This new organisation would be known as CHARIS (meaning Grace) and would be launched through the Pontifical Council for Laity, Family and Life, with a *'public juridical personality'*. In other words, the Catholic Charismatic Renewal would become an official Church organisation, able to speak in the name of the Church, and with a much higher profile than in the past.

CHARIS would exist to serve, advise and promote the whole Catholic Charismatic Renewal – it would not be an organisation with the authority to dictate what groups should say or do. No, its purpose would be to offer central support, encouragement, assistance and guidance as required and requested, on behalf of the Church. The structure would be simple – an International Council presided over by a Moderator with an office in Vatican premises in Rome, with Continental and National Councils of Communion. Whilst the members of these bodies would initially be appointed, as things became established and fully operational they would in future be elected.

This amazing decision made by Pope Francis gives full Church recognition to the worldwide Catholic Charismatic Renewal fifty two years after it began in 1967 among a group of students at Duquesne University. From now on, if people take a negative approach to the Renewal, rejecting, criticising or ignoring it, they will be denying an official Church organisation. In many ways, I see this as the culmination of what I have worked towards along with many other leaders worldwide since my personal baptism in the Holy Spirit in 1976, more than 40 years ago. It is certainly a sign of God's blessing – the full and official Church recognition of this amazing current of grace as vital for the life and health of the Church as we move forward in response to the universal call for a New Evangelisation. What are the recognised official objectives of CHARIS? They are clearly stated in the CHARIS Statutes and I am including them at the end of this chapter.

ECUMENICAL BY ITS NATURE
So a new phase begins in the relatively short life of the Catholic Charismatic Renewal, which is part of the much wider work of the Holy Spirit in world Christianity since the beginning of the twentieth century. We must give thanks for the vision and understanding of Pope Francis himself, a man publicly and unapologetically committed to the vital work of the Renewal in and beyond the Catholic Church, and who recognises the need for every Catholic man and woman to be open to receiving a new and personal outpouring of the Holy Spirit to equip them to live a much fuller life of faith as disciples of Jesus Christ. His personal priorities are baptism in the Holy Spirit for everyone; the vital work for the unity of all Christians from every part of the body of Christ; and a total commitment to helping the poor and needy wherever they may be. He fully supports the view of the late Cardinal Suenens that *'the Renewal is by its very nature ecumenical'*.

AN EXCITING FUTURE!
With the establishment of CHARIS at the heart of the Church, we are facing an exciting future. As things settle down, we may expect to be more involved in the main-stream life and activities of our Church. Our number one priority must remain baptism in the Holy Spirit for every single man and woman, and the vehicle we will often use to make this a reality wherever we are, will be the Life in the Spirit Seminars, the Gift, or any similar programmes the Holy Spirit may inspire in the days ahead. We are facing an exciting, challenging and ever-changing future. But we must always be on our guard to ensure that the greater involvement of the official Church does not cause us to neglect the on-going and never-ending personal and corporate challenges of the Holy Spirit, the key reason for this current of grace – the Charismatic Renewal.

The General Objectives of CHARIS
(taken from the official Statutes dated 6.12.2018)

a) To help deepen and promote the grace of baptism in the Holy Spirit throughout the Church.
b) To promote the exercise of charisms not only in Catholic Charismatic Renewal but also in the whole Church.
c) To encourage the spiritual deepening and holiness of people who live the experience of baptism in the Holy Spirit.
d) To encourage commitment to evangelisation, particularly through the new evangelisation and the evangelisation of culture, while respecting religious freedom.

e) To encourage co-operation between communities born
   from Catholic Charismatic Renewal, with a view to
   making the experience of particular communities
   available for the good of all.

f) To promote the ecumenical dimension of Catholic
   Charismatic Renewal and foster the commitment to
   serving the unity of all Christians.

g) To identify and promote specific topics that can help
   deepen the grace of Pentecost.

h) To encourage networking and cooperation between
   realities within Catholic Charismatic Renewal in the areas
   of formation, evangelisation etc.

i) To promote service of the poor and social action through
   the Catholic Charismatic Renewal.

j) To organise training and formation opportunities
   according to the needs expressed by the General
   Assembly.

k) To enable clerics and religious to deepen their experience
   of Catholic Charismatic Renewal, and to participate
   more fully in it.

l) To foster communion among persons involved in various
   realities within Catholic Charismatic Renewal; with
   ecclesial movements that do not refer to this current of
   grace; and with other Christian Churches and Communities,
   especially those living the experience of Pentecost.

m) To organise major events, colloquia, leaders' gatherings,
   in order to share and exchange the various experiences
   flowing from the Holy Spirit.

SEVEN

THE LORD SPEAKS

SINCE I WAS BAPTISED IN THE HOLY SPIRIT IN 1976, I have always believed that God speaks to us, often through the gift of Prophecy, and I have both given and received prophetic words quite often over the years. When Sue gave her life to the Lord in 1976, particularly inspired by the witness of a Baptist couple, Jim and Ina Hamilton, it brought me face to face with the fact that my faith was intellectual and not really alive. It had never touched my heart and affected my life. As explained in chapter 4, when Reverend Barry Kissell, the curate at St. Andrew's Church, Chorleywood, was given a prophetic word about this, he challenged me that I did not know how much God loved me personally and he prayed for me. The following day I experienced the amazing love God had for me for the first time and was baptised in the Holy Spirit. Then the Lord challenged me that I did not know His Word, so I spent two years reading, studying and praying through the whole Bible – the best investment of time I ever made.

THE SOUTHAMPTON CONFERENCE

In August 1979 I was persuaded by some members of the Holy Cross Prayer Group which we attended every week, to go with them to a five day Catholic Charismatic Conference at La Sainte Union College in Southampton. I was not particularly keen to go and Sue would not be able to come with me as she was in the late stages of pregnancy with Luke at the time, but they persisted and so I went. My initial experience there was not great. At the first session I found myself next to a man who insisted on grabbing my hand during the praise and worship and waving it above my head whilst talking to me in tongues!

After the evening Mass I was having a beer in the bar with our group (which included our good friend Sr. Ursula, one of the Holy Cross Sisters) before going to bed, and wondering if I would survive the next four days, when a priest walked past us. He stopped dead, turned, and said to me: *'What's the matter with you?'* *'Nothing'* I replied. *'Yes there is'* he said, *'You're not enjoying this – I'd better pray with you'*. So I put my beer down and followed him into another room – I think Sr. Ursula joined us to keep an eye on me!

'Lord, Bless Charles'

Now I had seen this priest praying with a woman earlier and she had fallen down under the power of the Holy Spirit, so I moved away to a safe distance from him and adopted a very unco-operative stance. He just smiled and said *'Lord, bless Charles'* and I found myself lying on the floor! He knelt down beside me and began to pray. He prayed in tongues, anointed me with blessed oil, and asked the Lord to reveal His plans to me and to equip me with all the gifts I might need for whatever I would be doing with Him in the future. He prayed for me for an hour – talking about me working for the Church, being in Rome, leading God's people and more. Then suddenly he was gone and I was alone on the floor. I stayed there for a while before quietly going to my room, where I opened my Bible and the Lord confirmed that He was sending me to His people. I prayed and fell asleep. The next morning I felt totally different, the Lord seemed to have transformed all the strange people into normal ones, and I greatly enjoyed the rest of the conference.

I owe a lot to this discerning Spirit-filled priest, Fr. Joe McShane, who was never afraid to do what he felt the Spirit was prompting him to do – even when this was likely on occasions to cause embarrassment to his Superiors, as I know it did!

'I WILL GIVE YOU...'
In the weeks that followed I began to receive invitations to speak to prayer groups and at Days of Renewal. Sue and I became part of the leadership of our Holy Cross Prayer Group, and I began serving in my parish of St. Joseph's in new ways, still often doing jobs no-one else was keen to do. Then in 1982 I was invited to become a member of the National Service Committee for the Catholic Charismatic Renewal in England and Wales, and the prophetic words I had received and continued to receive started becoming a reality in my life. At an ecumenical meeting for leaders a Pentecostal pastor came up to me and said he had a word for me from the Lord. *'I will give you a ministry to young people. You must not look for it, you must not try to make it happen, because at the right time I, the Lord, will deliver it to you'*. He walked away without any further explanation. He was in fact the same man who

later cast out the spirit of deafness from our son Luke, resulting in his total healing. I was not sure I wanted a ministry to young people but the Lord had said I should do nothing, so I just waited to see what would happen. Nearly four years later I received a telephone call from David Payne, the main leader of the Upper Room youth group in St. Albans. David and Tim Dawson had been baptised in the Holy Spirit, and with others including Sheila O'Donnell and Eamon Pugh had begun street evangelisation in St. Albans where they lived. A very large group of young people resulted, meeting frequently for praise, worship and prayer, which in due course became known as The Upper Room Community. Some of them came to the Southampton Conference, and when their leaders sought the Lord to know who should have oversight of what they were doing and help them pastorally, the Lord indicated me and Sue. Thus began my prophesied ministry to young people but it did not stop there. Some time later Damian Stayne, a university student, had requested a residence where a group of like-minded young Catholics could live together in community, but before agreeing to this the University Authorities required an older person to keep an eye on what they were doing. So Damian approached us to take on this responsibility for the embryonic youth community, which today is the well-known Cor et Lumen Christi Community. A third area of youth ministry came to us in the form of a school of evangelisation in Coventry, formed and led by Cormac O'Duffy, who felt he needed some help and guidance. After this I mentioned to the Lord that I felt we now had enough to keep us busy! Over time, of course, all three areas developed to the point where we were no longer needed on a regular basis, but by then I had also been instrumental in the employment of a full-time youth worker in our parish and I continued to have some responsibility in this for several years. One amazing thing occurred when we were on holiday in Majorca some years ago and as I was walking on the beach I sensed a prompting of the Holy Spirit. I felt He was asking me what ministries I had been given. I began to list them but omitted youth ministry as I thought that had come to an end. As I finished my list I sensed He said '*And..........?*', to which I responded that the main youth work had come to an end. '*Who said that?*' He asked.

DIOCESAN YOUTH
We returned home from our holiday and my fairly new Diocesan Bishop, Peter Doyle, telephoned to invite me for lunch. We enjoyed an interesting discussion about the diocese, and a few days later he contacted me to see if I would consider taking pastoral responsibility for our diocesan team of four full-time youth workers. Without hesitation I accepted, and when he asked why I did not want to pray about it, I explained that the Lord had spoken to me a couple of weeks earlier to prepare me. I had seven most enjoyable years serving in this capacity in my diocese.

PROPHETIC WORDS
At various points in my spiritual journey I have been given a prophetic word by someone, and without exception they have all been important moments. What was prophesied has come

to pass, although not necessarily immediately. We are often impatient people, keen to get on with things, but the Lord has His timing and we need to develop the gift of patience. I occasionally have a prophetic word for someone else and I have learned to have the confidence to deliver it when prompted to do so. I often receive reports some time later, confirming that what I prophesied had come to pass. The Lord uses this gift to prepare the way for what He is going to do, so that when the time comes we have the confidence to step out in faith and accept what He is saying.

A CHARISMATIC AND INSTITUTIONAL CHURCH
All the charismatic gifts of the Holy Spirit listed in *chapter 12 of Paul's first letter to the Corinthian Christians* are important and have a place in our daily lives. The Church confirmed this at the Second Vatican Council in section 12 of the document on the Church, *Lumen Gentium*. But the gift of Prophecy is often neglected, although it is essential for the life of the Church and I believe we need to pay special attention to it. When the Charismatic Renewal burst into the life of the Church in 1967, the authorities were able to quote *Lumen Gentium* as part of their discernment process, demonstrating thereby how the charismatic and the institutional parts of the Church are co-essential to her life.

EIGHT

SERVING MY LOCAL CHURCH COMMUNITY

THE LOCAL CHURCH – MY PARISH AND DIOCESE

WHEN MY FAITH CAME ALIVE IN 1976 I felt quite sure that I should start to play an active part in the life of my parish of St. Joseph's in Chalfont St. Peter, Buckinghamshire. It has been served for over 100 years by the Discalced Carmelites who bring their own particular and very acceptable spirituality to us. It was, and still is, a reasonable size parish, with a second smaller church in Denham village in addition to the main one. There is also St. Joseph's Combined School which takes pupils up to the age of twelve, and until it closed in 2008 the village Holy Cross Convent School took pupils up to A level and was partly boarding. The convent itself had up to ten sisters in the community, many of whom taught in the school. Since the school closed, about five of the sisters still live in a convent in the village. There is also a convent of Bridgettine Sisters in the parish at nearby Iver Heath, where they run a guest house close to Pinewood Studios. The Carmelites of course live as a community in the Priory alongside St. Joseph's church, where there are normally three or four of them in residence.

THE FIRST STEPS

The first thing I did in 1976 was to go to the parish priest and offer to do whatever parish job he found most difficult to cover. He was genuinely surprised at my offer, and asked if I would be willing to drive the mini-bus bringing some residents from the local epilepsy centre to the 11.00 a.m. Sunday Mass. This worked well for me as we had decided that as a family we would attend the 9.00 a.m. Family Mass which was the most lively, so I would be able to go on to the epilepsy centre from church. As we had four children, one girl and three boys, the Family Mass was excellent for us. Driving to the later 11.00 a.m. Mass I got to know my regular passengers from the epilepsy centre quite well, and before long I was taking them off for a drive around the area after Mass. Needless to say, the Parish Priest was delighted to have solved his transport problem, and began inviting me to join in other parish groups and activities. Although they would not say they were charismatic, the Carmelite clergy are men of prayer who are very open to the Holy Spirit and have always supported me in all my activities. We were also part of the Holy Cross Charismatic Prayer Group as mentioned in an earlier chapter.

In due course I was invited to join the St. Joseph's Parish Council, and because we had two young children we were also interested in the Parish Youth Club which was run by parents. There was considerable parental interest in having a full-time Parish Youth Worker, and the Parish Priest agreed that if we could raise the first year's salary and expenses, the parish would cover the costs from then on. We raised the money in three weeks, advertised, interviewed several applicants and appointed Mary Hughes, a qualified young teacher who had just returned from a spell working in Cameroon with the White Fathers and was exactly what we needed. She proved to be an amazing gift to the parish, stayed for about five years, and established our youth work on a firm foundation on which successive appointees were able to build.

THE NATIONAL PASTORAL CONGRESS
One of the big national church events that took place at the beginning of the 1980s was **The National Pastoral Congress.** Every parish had the opportunity to send delegates as part of their diocesan group and there was a period of diocesan preparation before the big event took place in Liverpool. All delegates had to choose to be part of one particular group which would be discussing a special topic before and during the Congress itself. I chose the Evangelisation Group, which proved to be the least popular both at diocesan level and at the Congress itself. This fact alone spoke volumes about the state of the Church at that time. We met several times before going to Liverpool, under the guidance of one of our diocesan priests, to prepare our thoughts on evangelisation under a variety of headings. I found myself leading our diocesan group under the priest, which involved writing up our evangelisation decisions for a diocesan paper which would also be sent to the Congress authorities before the event.

'THE CHURCH EXISTS TO EVANGELISE'
When the time came, we went up to Liverpool on a diocesan coach and were assigned accommodation with local families. I loved the Congress. We began in the famous Metropolitan Cathedral with the Archbishop, and watched a filmed message from Pope St. John Paul II – little did I dream that I would

have regular meetings with him in the future and come to know him quite well. In between plenary sessions we met according to our chosen topic with representatives from every diocese. We were mixed into small groups for discussion and produced reports which were collated by our Evangelisation Co-ordinator, Monsignor Paul Hypher. It is interesting to note that our topic of Evangelisation was again by far the least popular in the Congress and received the least attention from the organisers. This reflected the thinking of the average Catholic at the time in spite of Pope Paul VI's clear statement in his encyclical *'Evangelii Nuntiandi'* that *'the Church exists to evangelise'*. Our sector report at the end was well prepared and presented to the Congress by Monsignor Hypher, but it was hardly a surprise that it received the least Press interest or comment. Returning to the parish, our three delegates had the opportunity to give a short report to parishioners, and in late 1980 the full official document containing a review of The National Pastoral Congress with recommendations for the future, was published by the Bishops' Conference under the title *'The Easter People'* and contained many positive recommendations which make interesting reading today.

PARISH LIFE

I have very much enjoyed our parish life at St. Joseph's over the years and have never given a thought to going anywhere else. I have chaired the **Parish Council** on three separate occasions for three or four years each time, and have taken part in many fascinating groups and discussions about parish life, potential improvements and changes, the finances, new initiatives etc. The Carmelite Principal for our Province is based in Dublin and over the years I have come to know each of them and been invited on occasions for discussions with them. I was part of a small group invited to consider the future of **Boar's Hill**, the Carmelite Retreat Centre outside Oxford, an asset which still could in my opinion be more widely used.

We have had some wonderful Carmelite priests at St. Joseph's over the years, many of whom I count as personal friends, and there was a time when I was asked to consider training for the permanent diaconate. But I did not feel the Holy Spirit was leading me into this ministry. I have been a lay minister of the Eucharist since they were introduced, Sue and I have been readers at Mass for as long as I can remember, and regularly help with the annual preparation of our Confirmation candidates by speaking to them and to their parents about the Person of the Holy Spirit. From time to time we run the Life in the Spirit Seminars or The Gift in the Parish, and it's always a joy to see people coming alive in the love and power of the Spirit. I am currently one of our parish delegates to the local Chiltern Pastoral Area Council, and most courses are now usually run jointly and are open to all five parishes.

PERSONAL PRAYER MINISTRY
Recently we have begun to offer personal prayer ministry in the Oratory after the 9.00 a.m. Family Mass, and we had John and Gillian Ryeland from the London based Christian Healing Mission give us a day's teaching on 'Encounter Prayer'. The take-up after Mass is not huge, but two of us are available to

pray every week and people come with a variety of personal and family needs. I am quite sure this will grow steadily in the future. Looking back, I also remember with pleasure the years I spent taking a group of our parish young people who were not attending Catholic schools, for 'Sunday School'. The sessions took place on Saturdays for an hour or so and it was a joy to be able to introduce them to faith, to the Lord, and to pray for them.

SERVING OUR LOCAL CHURCHES

As I write all this I am very conscious that it sounds like a self-congratulatory account of achievements. This is absolutely not my intention – please believe me. But I feel it is important to emphasise the value of playing a really significant part serving in the life of our local church. It's all very well to do things in the wider Church but for almost all of us we live out our everyday lives of faith in our local parishes. If this is our situation, then it should be natural for us to play a really active part in parish life to whatever extent we are able. This is the reason behind these accounts of some of what I have done in my own parish of St. Joseph's, and I'm very aware of others too who serve tirelessly to make the experience of parish life positive and faith-building. At St. Joseph's I immediately think of three examples - Nan Jacobson who has enthusiastically led and inspired the children's and young people's choir for as long as I can remember, and Joan Barham, our Parish Pastoral Co-ordinator, who does a wonderful job and currently also chairs the Chiltern Pastoral Area Council, which represents five parishes. Nan's late husband, Jimmy, was also a tireless worker in St. Joseph's Parish, a wonderful servant of the Lord and an example to us all. He was the person who approached our Diocesan Bishop, Kevin McDonald (now an Archbishop), to set in motion the process that resulted in Pope St. John Paul II awarding me a Papal Knighthood of St. Gregory the Great (KSG) in July 2003.

CHURCHES TOGETHER

Wherever we live there are likely to be Protestant and other Evangelical churches and congregations, our brothers and sisters in Christ, with whom we will hopefully have good relationships, leading us to do things together. In the late 1980s our local Council of Churches often encouraged inter-denominational groups to gather in people's homes during Lent to follow the special Scripture-based programme which was produced annually in a different part of the world. We usually hosted a group in our home, and one year the suggestion was made that our local churches should consider the possibility of offering a joint mission to the area. I duly passed this suggestion on to the Council of Churches Committee, but heard nothing for several weeks. Then a letter came asking me to look into the possibility of putting on a joint mission and to let them know my findings.

A JOINT MISSION?

So I invited the leader of every local church to a meeting in our home to look into the possibility of doing a joint mission. I explained the idea and welcomed an honest and open discussion. After about half an hour I called a halt. It was already obvious that such an event was not possible – the relationships among the clergy were just not strong enough. There was mistrust, unspecified hints at sheep-stealing, and a simple lack of respectful understanding. I suggested we should meet together regularly for prayer, sharing and relationship building, and see where this took us. So a regular monthly meeting at our home began, and after fourteen months we reviewed our progress. It was amazing – our relationships had become warm and friendly, full of understanding and caring. We actually wanted the best for each other. In such a climate a joint mission was absolutely possible, so we decided to go ahead and look at what this might involve.

THE BIG TENT EVENT

We decided to go for a large marquee seating 1,000 people located on the Gerrards Cross Common, to aim for June in eighteen months time, to immediately start a programme of shared prayer in all our churches, to invite Scripture Union to lead the mission, to have a qualified team going into all the local schools, and to have main speakers from every denomination. There were the three local Anglican churches involved, the Catholic parish, the Baptist, Methodist and the United Reformed Church. Other churches just outside our designated area were also welcome to join us. There would be events going on all day in the marquee, starting with an early morning prayer meeting before people went to work, morning and lunchtime events, a late afternoon meeting for school children, and an open session every evening with a guest speaker. We had an excellent music ministry, good catering arrangements, a crèche and facilities for the disabled. Approval was obtained from the Parish Council to use the Common, traffic and parking questions were sorted out with the local police, and a marketing sub-group came up with the title **'The Big Tent Event'** with posters planned for everywhere. Each church trained counselling and prayer teams, we began inviting our guest speakers and planning a full programme with our local schools. I was elected to chair the Mission.

A Detailed Budget
Of course something like 'The Big Tent Event' costs money, and the participating churches all made their contributions according to their incomes and the sizes of their congregations. This meant that all our costs were covered without any complaints or disagreements. The success in this area was mainly due to the work of a well-qualified small financial committee, who efficiently prepared and explained a budget which covered all the costs in detail.

Positive Responses
The event itself was very popular and very successful. People came to every session, there were positive responses to every talk and people came forward for prayer or to talk to the response teams. I had been asked to work out how to guide people to a particular church team when they came forward. Not easy, but I came up with the following approach which was accepted by all the team and worked extremely well. A

man and a woman would stand at the front and those coming forward would go to one of them to be asked a few simple questions to ensure they were guided to the right team. **Firstly** – do you come from any particular church or church background? **Secondly** – is there any particular church you would like to be in touch with, or do you like the look of any particular local church? **Thirdly** – did someone bring you with them, and if so do you know which church they attend? **Finally** – would you be happy if I put you in touch with such and such a church? This system worked really well, and every church had new or returning members. Over the two weeks of the Mission about three hundred people in all responded at the sessions.

ANIMAL IMPERSONATIONS

The schools work was very encouraging and about 250 children came to the Big Tent after school every weekday afternoon, where there would be lively hymn and chorus singing, an appropriate drama from our invited Christian drama group, prayer, and a short message. The evangelical drama group were geared to events for schools and children, and performed some very lively sketches. I had invited Cardinal Basil Hume to be a main speaker, and somewhat to my surprise he accepted enthusiastically provided he could come to an afternoon session and address the children. Of course I agreed, so he came to our home for a cup of tea and a chat (he loved my system for helping those who came forward), after which we went across to the Big Tent as the children were arriving. The drama group was leading the afternoon and would introduce the Cardinal. They did an excellent drama which the children loved, there was some enthusiastic hymn singing, and then the leader of the drama group introduced Basil Hume by saying: *'Now boys and girls, we have a real treat for you – a Roman Catholic Cardinal! I know nothing about Cardinals, I don't know his wife's name or how many children he has, and for all I know he may come up now and do some farmyard animal impersonations for you!* But let's give a real Big Tent welcome to Cardinal Basil Hume!' The children shouted and cheered, the Cardinal gave me a long look and sauntered up to the microphone. Taking his cheeks between his fingers he did ducks going through a muddy farmyard, followed by a variety of superb animal impersonations! The children clapped, shouted and yelled with enthusiasm, the drama group leader and I just stood unable to believe our eyes. The Cardinal finished his impersonations, the children sat down, and looking warmly at them he said: *'I have only one thing to say to you – God is madly in love with each and every one of you. You may have been in trouble at school or at home, you may be having a bad day, but He just loves you anyway – totally and without conditions'.* You could have heard a pin drop as he went on to give a brilliant explanation of God's unconditional love. The children hung on every word, and when he finished they stood up shouting and cheering. Basil Hume left the platform and said to me *'How did you know that my party piece is animal impersonations?'* 'I didn't know that', I replied. 'So how did you know?', he asked the drama group leader. *'I had no idea'* he replied, *'it was just a joke'.* The Cardinal put his arm around my shoulders – *'Charles, you don't need to worry about anything – the Holy Spirit is clearly in charge of your mission'.*

THEIR UNITY HELD!

At the end of the two weeks the local press was totally positive. Their main questions at our morning press conferences had always been about our unity, which they did not think would survive two busy weeks with so much going on. But it did survive because of the strong relationships we had built up and the shared vision we had prayerfully adopted. So the headlines in the local papers all said the same thing: 'The Amazing Big Tent Event!' 'Their Unity Held!' and similar. Following the Mission we continued to meet as leaders for prayer at our home every month, and we still do, twenty eight years later. We also go on a two day retreat together every February, and have continued to put on events together during the year. For example, when the Olympic Games were in London, we invited everyone locally to the Gerrards Cross Common for the opening ceremony where we had a big screen, a Gospel choir, hamburgers and chips, and a cash bar. The local clergy all wore their clerical collars and mingled with the crowd, collecting rubbish and freely chatting. Several thousand people turned up and we had difficulty persuading the last ones to leave after midnight! During these London Olympics we had regular daily events on Chalfont St. Peter Common for different groups, and finished with the closing ceremony on a big screen with a similar number present as had attended the opening evening.

TOGETHER IN MISSION

We have learned the importance of the local churches moving out into the community **together,** giving a powerful witness to their faith and unity as they serve all the people. Perhaps the time is coming for another Big Tent or similar event, but the Lord will give the vision at the right time – we just have to remain open and attentive so that we don't miss it. We also need to know that there will be a lot of work involved and be prepared for this, remembering that the blessings will far outweigh the costs. In the meantime we have had a shared 24/7 Prayer Room in the centre of Chalfont St. Peter village to pray for our area, and we do various things together to keep our relationships strong.

THE DIOCESE
Every Catholic parish is part of a diocese, but apart from an occasional visit by the diocesan bishop – often for Confirmations – many parishioners have hardly any contact with their cathedral or diocesan officers. This is a pity, because the bishop has full authority over everything that goes on in his diocese and can in practice ignore decisions made by other Church authorities with which he is not in sympathy – how he runs his diocese is in *his* hands. A diocese will normally be a Charitable Trust with a Council of Trustees, and therefore accountable to the Charity Commissioners, but a bishop can choose to have only ordained clergy as his trustees or to have a mixture of clergy and laity. A wise bishop will always ensure he has people with financial, legal, administrative and educational experience among his trustees, and a good balance of younger and older, male and female etc. I have served as a trustee of my diocese for about ten years, which also involves being a member of the Finance Board, and I recently stepped

down to make room for a younger person. Our very popular Bishop, Peter Doyle, had offered his resignation when he reached 75 years of age in late 2019, and Canon David Oakley, who was serving as the Rector of Oscott Seminary, was appointed to succeed him taking over in March 2020. He has been a personal friend for a number of years, so I had been praying that he would be our new Bishop in Northampton Diocese, as I know he will make an excellent leader. I'm now looking ahead with confident enthusiasm!

TRUSTEES

The responsibility of a Trustee covers everything that goes on in the diocese, and carries all the financial affairs of the parishes, the maintenance and use of all buildings, accommodation for clergy and diocesan employees, as well as education, general safety issues, and provision for trainee and retired clergy. It is not a role to be undertaken lightly. The trustees receive regular reports from all the central activities in the diocese – education and schools, employment, safe-guarding, youth ministry, maintenance of buildings, matters relating to clergy plans for expansion and contraction, spiritual training programmes, financial and legal matters, and all major diocesan events. It is very likely that a trustee will be involved in one or more sub-committees and in a variety of meetings. It is demanding but rewarding work. In the current situation, diocesan trustees also receive confidential reports on any instances of alleged sexual abuse by clergy, current or historic, and are available to give advice to their bishop if needed. I also enjoy being a member of the Northampton Diocesan Ecumenical Commission, which plans practical ways we can work together with other churches and fellowships in the Diocese, and I will continue to be a member of this important Commission.

COMMITTED CHRISTIANS

In this chapter I have tried to give a simple account of what might be involved in playing an active part in a parish and diocese, with some rather exceptional ecumenical opportunities like The Big Tent Event, purely to show the variety and content of involvement available to us. It is not meant to be totally comprehensive – far from it – but is based on my own experience of what is possible when we commit ourselves to serving in those areas and communities where we live out our Christian lives. The most important point to make is that each of us has the opportunity to play a part in the life of the local church. There are always areas where help is needed, and this is all part of what it means today to be a committed Christian. Baptism in the Holy Spirit is intended to equip us to play a full part in the life of the Church at every level – not just at charismatic events. In my view, we should step forward and offer to serve rather than just wait to see if we are invited.

NINE

THE WIDER COMMUNITY

I N THE EARLY 1980s I RECEIVED AN INVITATION to become a
member of the National Service Committee (NSC) for the
Catholic Charismatic Renewal in England and Wales,
which at the time also meant automatically becoming a Trustee
of the CREW Trust, a registered charity formed by the NSC to
take responsibility for the finances which were needed for the
NSC's ministry. At the time, the NSC served England and
Wales, but a few years later the Welsh members left to form an
NSC for Wales, and this is still the situation today.

PROMOTING THE RENEWAL
The NSC had been appointed at the big Charismatic
Conference at Hopwood Hall in the late 1970s, thereby
confirming the important role of the group of leaders who had
come together to put on the Conference. A few other countries,
notably the USA, had formed national committees which went
under various titles, but all shared the same general aims of
promoting, encouraging, developing and serving this amazing
outpouring of the Holy Spirit known as the Catholic
Charismatic Renewal, which was rapidly becoming
established in almost every country in the world. The first NSC
Chairman for England and Wales was Bob Balkam, an
American who had been baptised in the Holy Spirit in the USA
before being posted to England by his employers,
Redemptorist Publications, to promote the sales of their

Catholic books. We owe a great deal to Bob, who brought together some of the early leaders in England and Wales and organised some of the first events and gatherings. He identified the key leaders and held meetings to plan how best to serve and promote this amazing outpouring of the Holy Spirit which was already transforming hundreds of lives. This is how, with the help of a small group of leaders, the Hopwood Conference took place in Manchester. It proved to be a key event, formally recognising a National Service Committee with the aim of promoting the CCR in England and Wales, with Bob as Chairman.

ENCOURAGING LOCAL EVENTS

I felt honoured to be invited to become a member with some great servants of God including Fr. Ian Petit OSB, Sr. Mary Peter Scanlan, Fr. Michael Gwinnell, and Fr. Sean Conaty among others. There was a small office in London, and the Good News was a simple newsletter for which Fr. Derek Lance became responsible. We met as an NSC about four times a year, usually staying overnight, with Bishop Langton Fox who was our Episcopal Advisor, appointed by the Bishops' Conference. You may have noticed that the early NSC members were mainly priests or sisters, as lay people were not used to taking on spiritual leadership - but this soon changed. One of the early decisions of the NSC was not to organise big national conferences on a regular basis, but to encourage regional gatherings around the country. The formation and encouragement of local prayer group leaders was seen as very important, as prayer groups were by far the most common expression of the CCR, supported by regional Days of Renewal. The NSC saw its primary mission as encouraging and promoting these new expressions of spiritual life, whilst facilitating and resourcing the Life in the Spirit Seminars far and wide. These originated in the USA and offered a series of sessions explaining life in the Spirit, culminating in prayers for baptism in the Holy Spirit for all the participants. The Good News quickly expanded into a proper magazine, edited by Fr. Derek Lance, but it was then taken on as a full-time ministry by trained journalist Kristina Cooper, who remained as editor until February 2020 when the final issue was published. During those 35 years she did an amazing job producing and promoting an excellent magazine which presented all that the Holy Spirit was doing among a wide variety of individuals, groups and organisations both nationally and internationally. She enjoyed the committed support of the NSC and CREW Trust in all that she did over those 35 years and devoted her life to this remarkable ministry, which meant that Good News was known around the world for its consistently excellent articles and news reporting. Both Kristina and the magazine will be greatly missed.

THE IMPORTANCE OF ECUMENISM

My early meetings as an NSC member focused on finding ways to support and develop all that was happening in the CCR, to establish Diocesan Service Committees to work locally, to provide teaching and Bible study resources, and to develop the Good News Magazine into the major source of information about events all over the country and the recognised channel for teaching on life in the Holy Spirit. One decision was made by the NSC about which I had my doubts – it was decided to specifically dedicate the Catholic Charismatic Renewal in England and Wales to Our Lady. I felt that this would cause problems with some of our carefully developed ecumenical relationships. This proved to be what happened, and some of our strongest Anglican supporters wrote to express their real concerns at this development which they saw as immediately problematic for them. Some of the NSC felt that it was simply their problem and not ours, something they just had to get over, but I was well aware that it had been a very unhelpful thing to do when building unity was, and remains, such a key feature of this new life in the Spirit. So I committed myself to working harder than ever to build bridges with all our Protestant, Independent, and Pentecostal brothers and sisters. Cardinal Suenens had emphasised that the Catholic Charismatic Renewal was *'by its very nature ecumenical'* and I totally endorse this.

The CREW Trust

In 1978 it had been decided to set up an independent charity to look after the financial affairs of the NSC and to serve the whole CCR by handling all the financial needs and bequests that were referred to them. All the NSC members were registered as the Trustees of the charity because in law the Trustees were responsible for making the financial decisions and it was therefore more straightforward if the two bodies were one and the same. The charity was called the CREW Trust – Charismatic Renewal in England and Wales. At the time there was only a very small sum of money in the Trust, so questions of investment skills, good financial management etc did not arise. Not all the NSC members wanted to be Trustees as they felt ill-equipped for this responsibility, but they agreed to serve as there was little need for any financial expertise. Some years later, however, it was decided to establish a fund to raise money which would cover the expenses of the Chairman and any members who might incur costs in representing the NSC at special events or might need compensation for loss of income. A very generous loan of £200,000 was made to this fund and it was proposed that the Chairman should receive fees from this fund in compensation for loss of income when engaged on NSC business. At the time a Trustee could not receive fees from the charity, so the NSC Chairman ceased to be a Trustee and one or two outsiders with financial expertise were invited to serve as Trustees, one of them as Chairman. The Trustees adopted the general practice of giving their advice to the NSC and then leaving the final decision in their hands. For their part, the NSC took seriously the advice of the Trustees on all financial and administrative matters and followed their recommendations.

NSC CHAIRMAN
In 1985 Bob Balkam returned to the USA and I was elected Chairman in his place. My first recommendation was to hold a National Conference for Leaders, which took place in Birmingham in 1987 and was generally seen as a great success. Relationships were established, mutual understanding was shared, delegates had a common vision and sense of purpose

as part of something amazing that God was doing, and friendships grew. Wales had decided to establish a separate NSC for their country and followed this course of action, but their finances remained under CREW Trust. For some years the Chair of the Welsh NSC came as a welcome guest to the English NSC meetings, but this practice gradually declined. I think it is probably something that may be revived.

A Life Member

My years as NSC Chairman saw a range of events and activities take place at local and national levels – the FIRE Rallies from the USA in London and Manchester, the continuing development of the Good News Magazine, the employment of staff and establishment of offices, the institution of Catholic Evangelisation Services with David Payne which led to Alpha for Catholics in 1996 followed by CaFE (Catholic **Faith** Exploration) and the extensive programme of wide-ranging courses for groups and parishes, the Patmos Retreats etc. In 2003 a small NSC Committee was set up to plan for my successor as Chair after almost 20 years service, and recommended a change over a 12 month period. However, the next NSC meeting decided there was no reason not to go ahead with this and Michelle Moran was chosen to take over with immediate effect. I was then appointed a Life Member of the NSC and have remained an active participant in support of the elected members, currently under the gifted chairing of Maria Heath.

THE NATIONAL SERVICE COMMITTEE

A good NSC will serve and reflect the CCR in the area it covers. To do this well, it will be made up of leaders with a variety of gifts and experience – in teaching and training, organisation and administration, the prophetic, prayer ministry, Scripture projects, communication, evangelisation and outreach. They will also represent different expressions of the CCR – communities, special ministries, prayer initiatives, ministry to young people, social care, and more. In a variety of ways the English NSC has covered these areas, with the Network serving young people through the Ascent formation programme, the encouragement of current forms of worship, evangelisation projects and a variety of events and activities which bring young people together, thereby building strong, committed relationships. The establishment of CHARIS will ensure the continuation of this important service with a higher status, and the National Service Committee will probably become the National Service of Communion with some more members.

GOOD RELATIONSHIPS

A key responsibility for every NSC is to encourage and develop local leadership at parish level and in dioceses and regions. My experience of our English NSC is that by and large we are doing this to good effect but it demands constant vigilance and at present we are putting more energy into building up diocesan and regional leadership. At the same time there is a need to develop and maintain good relation-ships in a whole variety of ways – with other denominations, with the Catholic hierarchy, with other movements in the Church, with special ministries serving a wide range of needs in society at home and abroad. Some years ago we held a special conference in Birmingham for CCR leaders in England, Scotland, Ireland and Wales which we called The Newman Consultation. Our main speaker was Fr. Raniero Cantalamessa OFM. We also invited a number of leaders from other churches and ministries to build greater unity among us all. The fruit of this Consultation has not been the establishment of a range of activities and events – that was never the aim – but it has led to regular meetings between members of the four NSCs involved, for fellowship, building understanding and relation-ships, sharing what the Spirit is saying and doing, along with prayer, the development of good ecumenical relationships, and seeking vision for the way ahead.

All in all, I feel that our English NSC has a good vision and does a great job in fulfilling its mission to serve and promote the CCR. It remains a privilege to be a member, and we can now look forward to the new life and empowerment that CHARIS will bring us.

A MOMENT OF OPPORTUNITY

Important initiatives are not, of course, restricted to the National Service Committee. A good example is **'A Moment of Opportunity'**, an annual two day gathering of about 70 invited Charismatic leaders to share fellowship, to build relationships, to seek the Lord together, to minister to each other, to share what the Holy Spirit is doing, and to hear from inspirational speakers both Catholic and from other churches and fellowships. Inspired by Damian Stayne, founder of the Cor et Lumen Christi Community, a small committee came into being to make 'A Moment of Opportunity' a reality, consisting of Damian with NSC members and younger leaders, which I was invited to chair with Sue looking after the administration. We are now in our seventh year, and it has proved to be a very creative and inspirational gathering of a wide variety of Charismatic leaders.

TEN

INTERNATIONAL CATHOLIC CHARISMATIC RENEWAL (ICCRS)

WHEN I WAS BAPTISED IN THE HOLY SPIRIT IN 1976 I knew nothing of local, national or international Charismatic Renewal Service Committees, tasked with encouraging, promoting, resourcing and guiding the many expressions of the worldwide CCR. I gradually became aware that we had a National Service Committee for England and Wales, but I knew little of its purpose or membership. I soon learned of the events which had occurred at the Duquesne Weekend in the USA in 1967, and that what I had experienced was basically just the same as these students had experienced – a sovereign, life-changing out-pouring of the Holy Spirit. As I explain in my testimony, I had been well formed in Catholic teaching by the Jesuits, even though I had missed the central point of it all – a personal living relationship with our Lord and Saviour Jesus Christ. So in 1976 my training led me to look at Church teaching to find out what it said about what I had experienced. I found section 12 in the document *Lumen Gentium* from Vatican II, where the charismatic gifts are explained and endorsed, and this led me to the Letters of St. Paul in the New Testament, which I also found helpful and reassuring. So I accepted that what I had experienced was in line with Church teaching and with Scripture, and should be part of the experience of every Christian, whether Catholic or Protestant. As I then looked at how this was being taught, explained and promoted, I began to understand the role of NSCs and to follow the journey of acceptance by the Church of what had become known as the Catholic Charismatic Renewal. An international office had been established by Cardinal Suenens in Belgium which had later moved to Rome into convent premises, and was now led by a small international committee still under the benevolent eye of Cardinal Suenens, one of the architects of Vatican II.

THE INTERNATIONAL CATHOLIC CHARISMATIC RENEWAL COUNCIL
The Council of the International Catholic Charismatic Renewal Office (ICCRO) was made up of 15-20 representatives of the worldwide Renewal. These representatives were lay people, priests, deacons, religious and usually one or two bishops, coming from different continental areas and particular expressions and ministries of the Catholic Charismatic Renewal. They met once or twice a year, usually in Rome, and sub-committees were elected with particular areas of responsibility and service. The ICCRO Council organised occasional meetings for leaders as well as large open conferences. As Chairman of the English NSC I began to attend these events, and as the organisers got to know me I was invited to serve in different ways during the events themselves. At an open conference in Rome in 1988 I was surprised to be contacted by the personal secretary of Cardinal Suenens, Fr. Wilfrid Brievens, who invited me to a private meeting for coffee with the Cardinal at his Rome residence. We met and had a very open conversation about the CCR and my interest and involvement in it. Rather to my surprise he expressed interest in my marriage to a Protestant wife and how

we handled our differences, but the whole conversation which lasted about an hour and a half was both interesting and positive.

A Surprising Invitation
I returned to the conference and was met by the Director of ICCRO with an invitation to consider becoming a member of the Council as a representative of Northern Europe. Only then did the penny drop, as I realised I had just passed my interview with Cardinal Suenens! I felt it was right to accept the invitation, recognising that I would be attending one or two Council meetings a year, usually lasting several days, and that as I lived in Europe I would also be likely to come to the Rome office from time to time. By the time I went home from the conference I had met all my fellow councillors and heard more about the work involved.

Council Meetings
My first Council meeting was more formal than I was expecting. We sat around a large table and after a short time of prayer began to address our agenda under the efficient chairmanship of Fr. Diego Jaramillo from Colombia, the ICCRO President. I felt I would certainly have things to contribute at the Council meetings, but I had no idea how quickly this would prove to be the case.

Our Papal Advisor
Bishop Paul Cordes, the Vice-President and Secretary of the Pontifical Council for Laity, was the personal appointee of

Pope John Paul II as his advisor to the Council of ICCRO and to the CCR. Bishop Cordes had decided not to attend the Council meeting at all, because he had the impression that the Council members and the ICCRO office staff had not been consulting him or seeking his views on any of their projects, and did not value his input and advice. This was obviously an embarrassing position for him when the Holy Father asked him what was going on in the CCR and in the ministry of the ICCRO Council. I don't think ICCRO had intentionally been ignoring him, but had probably not seen a need to consult him. They now of course recognised that this was an error on their part which needed to be resolved and a good relationship with Bishop Cordes restored. In discussion it was decided that as I had not been party to any of this, I would be the best person to talk to Bishop Cordes and to restore the relationship. I was duly given this responsibility, and the fact that I lived in Europe would make it easy for me to travel to Rome during this process. So I was given the title of 'Vice-President of ICCRO' to indicate that I was an important member of the Council and had the authority to resolve the difficulties which had arisen. When the Council meeting ended, I therefore contacted Bishop Cordes and we arranged to meet at his residence before I left Rome.

RESTORING RELATIONSHIP

Bishop Cordes lived in an apartment inside Vatican City, so we met there the following evening. He greeted me very warmly and after a short prayer opened a bottle of German Riesling and asked me what had attracted me to the Charismatic

Renewal. I shared my personal testimony very fully, answered his questions, and then asked how he came to be serving as a bishop in Rome and the number two official at the Council for Laity. His story was fascinating, and included the fact that when he was a priest serving in Germany, the bishops had asked him to be the travelling companion of Cardinal Wojtyla of Poland when he made a 12 day tour of the German dioceses. It would not be appropriate to share his personal story here, but he had established a close relationship with the Polish Cardinal, and was later studying in Rome at the time Wojtyla was elected Pope, shortly after which Cordes was ordained a bishop and then appointed to serve at the Council for Laity. He and I established a good personal relationship and enjoyed dinner together in his favourite local restaurant. Over the following months I travelled to Rome several times to continue our discussions, a good relationship with the Council and staff of ICCRO was restored, and I was able to make a positive report to the ICCRO President and Councillors. The Director of the ICCRO office, Fr. Ken Metz, then joined me in meeting Bishop Cordes and a good pattern of regular contact was established.

THE NEW COUNCIL PRESIDENT
I travelled to Rome the day before our next Council meeting, and this proved to be very fortunate as a telephone call came through from our President, Fr. Diego Jaramillo, to say that he would not be able to come to Rome. In fact he tendered his resignation from the Council, because his bishop had suddenly asked him to take on some major new diocesan responsibilities

which would mean that he would not have any time available for his ICCRO responsibilities. When we assembled as the Council the following day, I was asked as Vice-President to chair the meeting until we elected a new President a couple of days later. When the election took place, two candidates were proposed, and I was elected the new President with the full endorsement of Bishop Cordes who then joined our meeting.

You will appreciate that this was not something I had ever thought might happen, so it took me completely by surprise. But I came to see it as the Lord's will for me and therefore something for which He would equip me and guide me. I had the total backing of my fellow Councillors and of the office staff, and the assurance of their full support for whatever I felt might need to be changed as we moved ahead, blessed by our new relationship with Bishop Cordes. I chaired the Council meeting to the best of my ability, after which I went to the ICCRO offices and took my place in the elegant room assigned to the President, with its beautiful mahogany desk and other furniture. The only thing on my desk was a polished telephone – not a piece of paper in sight.

A Surprising Telephone Call

As I sat there wondering what I should now be doing as ICCRO President, the telephone rang. I answered it and a polished English male voice enquired if he had the pleasure of speaking to the newly elected President of ICCRO. He informed me that he was the British Ambassador to the Holy See, John Broadley, that he and his wife Jane were resident in

Rome in an official house, and that he expected I might be
sitting at my desk wondering what I should now be doing in
my new position! He invited me to their house for dinner, sent
a chauffeur driven car to collect me, and I discovered to my
delight that he and his wife were committed charismatic
Anglicans! We began our evening with praise and prayer,
enjoyed a lovely dinner, and fixed a date for another dinner to
which he would invite other guests I might like to meet –
Cardinals and key Press contacts. We became good friends,
and John and Jane supported me enormously, even to the
extent that Sue and I helped by co-hosting a summer garden
party in celebration of Queen Elizabeth's official birthday the
following June, to which Cardinals, Bishops, Ambassadors,
and important people from the Media all came. This served to
confirm that the Lord was very much behind my election as
the new President of ICCRO with an office in the Vatican,
regular contact with Pope John Paul II, and now the friendship
and help of the British Ambassador.

THE FAMILY FIRST

It was not practical for us to consider moving to Rome as a
family for a variety of reasons. Most important was the fact
that we had four children, all at different stages in their
education, and to try to continue this in Rome was unrealistic
and would be unfair to them Then of course I was still working
as Managing Director of the UK sales organisation of a
multinational Swedish company in the forestry and paper
industry, and so I remained UK based, travelling to Rome and
other places as necessary. The fact that I had seven weeks

holiday and could take extra days occasionally by agreement also helped a lot.

POPE ST. JOHN PAUL II

My first meeting with Pope St. John Paul II was memorable and took place shortly after my election as ICCRO President.

One of many meetings during the 1990s with
Pope St. John Paul II in the Vatican

He told me that since his early teenage years he had prayed to the Holy Spirit daily, on the advice of his father, for help with whatever challenges he faced, and he assured me of his support and availability. He suggested that I let his secretary know when I would be in Rome, and from time to time I received an invitation to join him for his early morning private

Mass in his apartments, after which we would have a short conversation about how things were going and what important things were happening. I was always welcome to contact him through his secretary if anything particularly significant was happening. At least once a year he met with the full ICCRO Council, when I would give a report on what was happening, to which he would respond. He had a good sense of humour which I experienced on a number of informal occasions. I found the fact that every morning he spent an hour in private prayer in his chapel between six and seven o'clock when he celebrated Mass very inspiring, and he brought Romans 8:26 to life: *'the Spirit Himself intercedes for us with groans that words cannot express'.*

'PRAY FOR ME'

When he left us after a meeting he would always say *'Pray for me'* and when I said this to Sue on one occasion she asked me why we had not prayed for him then and there? This thought stayed with me, and the next time I met him with some of the Council he was very exhausted having just returned from a trip overseas. When he said *'Pray for me'* I asked if he would like us to do that before he left, and although he looked a bit surprised, he agreed and we gathered round him, I laid hands on him, we sang and prayed in tongues, and there was a prophetic word. He was visibly moved and blessed, with his head bowed and his eyes closed. As we finished praying, he did not immediately move and then slowly opened his eyes, warmly thanking each of us. He began to leave but turned back to thank us again, assuring us he felt really blessed.

Finally he left, late for his next appointment, and a few minutes later his secretary returned to tell me off for making him late but also to thank me and to assure me how important this had been for the Pope. Apparently no-one had laid hands on him as I had just done since he became Pope! When I think back, I realise what a privilege it was to pray over a Pope who was later to be canonised, and how grateful I am to have had such an opportunity.

PRIVATE PAPAL MASSES
From time to time the Council also received an invitation to join the Pope for his private morning Mass, and his secretary always added that we should be ourselves – charismatic. So we would sing in tongues, have an occasional prophetic word, and one of us would read the first Scripture. After Mass, John Paul II would spend a few precious minutes informally chatting with us before going for his breakfast followed by a succession of appointments and meetings.

STATUTES FOR THE COUNCIL
I felt that my first important task after being elected President of ICCRO was to obtain official Vatican recognition for the Council and our work. The Pontifical Council for the Laity would be open to approving Private Statutes if we had them drawn up, and Bishop Cordes assured me of his full support in this task. So I began the work with the help of a small sub-committee of Council members, and we asked three Canon Lawyers to work on drawing up appropriate Statutes. Kevin Ranaghan prepared a pre-amble which explained the nature

of the Catholic Charismatic Renewal and what the Council did, whilst Bishop Cordes set in motion the Vatican preparation of a Decree which would express their formal approval. Cardinal Ratzinger accepted the final Statutes which were then officially presented to us in September 1993 by Cardinal Pironio, the President of the Pontifical Council for Laity. The Decree and the Statutes gave formal approval to the Council of ICCRO and our work in communicating, promoting and advising the worldwide CCR. This did not give approval to every local expression of the CCR – that was in the hands of the local hierarchy – but of course the Vatican would not have granted Statutes to the Council if they had not approved of the worldwide Catholic Charismatic Renewal.

A MORE ACCURATE TITLE
Our title, ICCRO, was changed to ICCRS – International Catholic Charismatic Renewal Services – as this more accurately described our function and purpose. The Vatican approval of our Statutes was, in my opinion, a very important step forward for the International Catholic Charismatic Renewal and for the work and service of the Council.

ELEVEN

A JOURNEY IN FAITH - ALL OVER THE WORLD

MY TEN YEARS AS ICCRS PRESIDENT were exciting, challenging, full of amazing opportunities and very personally rewarding. I visited more than sixty-five countries around the world from Australia to Finland, meeting thousands of those involved with the CCR in all sorts of different ways. I met quite a number of political and business leaders as well, of course, as Cardinals, Bishops, clergy and religious in various countries. Sometimes Sue was able to come with me, and I built up a fascinating picture of this remarkable move of the Holy Spirit. Cardinal Suenens had originally called it 'Catholic Pentecostalism' but this risked confusion with the many expressions of the Pentecostal Churches and so it was soon changed and linked to the charisms by its new title 'Catholic Charismatic Renewal'.

ICCRS CONFERENCES AND RETREATS
ICCRS put on a variety of conferences, retreats and other events during my Presidency, and it was certainly evident that all over the world the Spirit was moving. Here are descriptions of just a few of these events. Important among them was a memorable retreat in Assisi given by Fr. Raniero Cantalamessa, the Preacher to the Papal Household appointed by Pope John Paul II. Fr. Ken Metz, ICCRS Director, had managed to borrow the Tent of Unity owned by a French ecumenical organisation, and had obtained permission to erect it on the top of the hill

of Assisi. This allowed our international retreatants to walk up
the hill silently every morning, to enjoy an exuberant time of
praise and worship in the tent, followed by input from Fr.
Raniero, reflected upon in silence. It was an excellent week and
we were delighted that some of our friends in leadership in
other parts of the body of Christ had accepted our invitation
to join us. They included Canon Michael Harper from the
Anglican Church and Pentecostal Pastor Vinson Synan.

The Assisi Retreat took place during the time Pope John Paul
II was on holiday at Castel Gandolfo, and our request for an
audience at the end of our week had received a negative
response from the bishop responsible for his holiday diary. But
we persisted, largely through our Polish Council member,
Bishop Dembowski, a friend of the Pope. At the last minute
we received a message welcoming us to visit the Pope when
we left Assisi, so we hastily hired the large number of buses
necessary to transport us all to Castel Gandolfo on our way to
Rome and the international airports. Sitting on the bus I hastily
put together a few thoughts in case I was invited to address
the Holy Father.

ENCOURAGING WORDS
On arrival at Castel Gandolfo we assembled in the courtyard,
and the bishop secretary sought me out to express his irritation
that we had somehow got to the Pope, who had then asked
him to arrange the meeting. But he assured me that John Paul
II would remain on the balcony and would greet us briefly
from up there. We began to sing songs of praise when to my

surprise I saw the Holy Father coming down the steps into the courtyard. He greeted me warmly and asked me to introduce him to the front row, which included our ecumenical guests. In fact he personally greeted far more people than just the front row before taking his seat and inviting me to speak. After I had spoken he responded very positively and partly spontaneously, congratulating us on choosing Fr. Raniero to lead our retreat. Our delegates were delighted, and went off on their journeys home with the Pope's encouraging words in their ears.

A GATHERING IN THE HOLY LAND

Another special international conference took place in the Holy Land with over 2,000 participants, including groups from African and Latin American countries. The whole event, a pilgrimage plus a conference, was enormously helped by Council member Henri Lemay from Canada, who spent some months living in Jerusalem to oversee the preparations. The gathering began with a pilgrimage travelling around the Sea of Galilee, visiting churches and special sites, and included a healing service on the shore attended by a large number of local people and led by Fr. Emiliano Tardiff. This included some very powerful ministry to many of the local attendees. Then the main conference took place in Jerusalem itself, but we travelled by coach to Bethlehem for the opening evening, passing through the Israeli check-point in both directions as Bethlehem is in the Palestinian area. In fact I had received a telephone call from Yasser Arafat, the Palestinian leader, to say that he was planning to come to Bethlehem to welcome us.

Now this could have been a problem, because we had gone to great lengths to avoid all politics, and had already declined to be welcomed to Jerusalem by a high-ranking Israeli government official. So Yasser Arafat joining us in Bethlehem would be an embarrassment. I tried to explain this, but when I stood up in Manger Square in Bethlehem to thank the Christian mayor for his welcome, I had no idea if Arafat was going to turn up. As I spoke there were noises behind me, and since my words were being consecutively translated for the local people, my Vice-President Kevin Ranaghan appeared at my side and during the translation of each sentence he informed me that I had no need to worry. Apparently they were simply unfurling a big Palestinian poster behind me, and on the opposite side of the square they were lowering from the top of the buildings a massive photograph of Yasser Arafat. I could relax – he was obviously not coming in person!

ESCORTED BY A PLATOON OF INFANTRY

I should point out that our event was taking place during a period of high tension in the whole area, and most pilgrimages and foreign visitors had cancelled their trips, so to have a big international group like ours was very unusual and attracted the positive attention of the authorities everywhere. The remainder of our event was in Jerusalem, a combination of excellent teaching and visits to some of the holy places. Apart from the slightly unnerving fact that we were being escorted everywhere by a platoon of Israeli infantry, everything passed off normally.

BUILDING RELATIONSHIPS WITH MESSIANIC JEWISH LEADERS
At the end of the conference some of the ICCRS Council were
to spend a day with a group of Messianic Jewish Leaders
based in Israel. The intention was to increase our mutual
understanding and to build good relationships, but the
meeting started unpromisingly. They gave us their names but
were unwilling to explain anything about their fellowships
or ministry, so I silently asked the Holy Spirit for His help.
'Peter Hocken' He said in my heart. Now Fr. Peter had not
been able to come to Jerusalem but he was of course a great
friend to the Messianic Jews, so at the first opportunity I
referred to '*my good friend Peter Hocken*' and gave them his
greetings. The result was amazing. They asked me about my
relationship with Peter and if other people in the room also
knew him. Then they began to share freely and openly – any
friends of Peter's were their friends too! We had a fascinating
time together and established really good contact.

HEALINGS AT A CONFERENCE IN ITALY
Another ICCRS conference which made a deep impression on
me took place near the shrine to Padre Pio at San Giovanni
Rotondo. Sr. Nancy Kellar was the ICCRS Director at the time
and had been greatly helped in the preparations for this event
by Claude Lopez and his wife Miralda from Australia. Claude
himself had earlier been a very key person at the ICCRS office
in Rome, a former Director, and often came back from
Melbourne to help when we were putting on big international
events. On this occasion, in addition to the conference itself,
we were holding a big rally in the local stadium with a focus

on healing for all those who lived in the area. The local bishop was not initially very helpful, but when we explained that we intended to make a generous donation to his diocese, his attitude changed and he encouraged us warmly.

Oreste Pesare

His personal secretary was Oreste Pesare, a leader of a local charismatic covenant community. Oreste helped us enormously, and in fact when Sr. Nancy Kellar later returned to the USA, Oreste became the new Director of ICCRS, a position he held to great effect until the arrival of CHARIS in 2019 – a period of more than twenty-five years. When we employed him, Oreste spoke very little English, so Claude Lopez invited him to Australia to remedy this situation. I was a bit concerned that he would return with some 'Australian English' but the Lord was clearly very much with him, and I was delighted when he returned after some weeks speaking remarkably good and fluent 'normal English'!

A Few Hundred Extra Tickets

One of the little Italian 'challenges' that faced us was that someone had printed an unknown number of extra tickets for the Stadium event, resulting in the need for closed circuit television to reach at least some of those who had bought tickets but were unable to gain entry to the Stadium. However, it proved to be a great occasion with reports of many healings when Fr. Emiliano Tardiff ministered, with warm welcomes to the event from the local bishop, from myself and Sr. Nancy, encouraging words from Fr. Raniero and others, and with huge interest from the local media.

THE NATIONAL PRAYER BREAKFAST IN MANILA

In addition to those mentioned here, ICCRS organised other conferences and retreats, and in my capacity as President I visited many countries. One example that has stayed with me was a trip to the Philippines in 1995. Much to my surprise, I received an invitation from the Justice Minister in Manila to address their annual Prayer Breakfast which was attended by the President, the Cardinal, members of the Government, and by leaders in business, the professions, politics and the Church. Hearing about this, my friend and ICCRS Council member Fr. Bart Pastor, immediately invited me to come for a week before the Breakfast to speak to some CCR groups and to lead a special retreat. Sue had been included in the official invitation, so we ministered together at the events Fr. Bart had planned, leading up to the National Prayer Breakfast at the Sheraton Hotel in Manila.

A SMART OUTFIT

When we checked into the Sheraton Hotel the evening before the Breakfast, a note awaited me from the Justice Minister, welcoming us and telling me that I would find something in my wardrobe I might like to wear. We went up to our very pleasant room and in the wardrobe was a good quality white, formal, high necked, traditional Philippino shirt, with a short-sleeved vest to wear underneath it. It fitted well, so the next morning I put it on instead of my dark suit and we went down to the large meeting room for the Breakfast. The Justice Minister was awaiting us, and he showed me onto the platform where I would be seated for breakfast between the

President and the Cardinal. He also introduced me to my heavily armed bodyguard who would be at my side wherever I went. The many guests began to arrive and at 0745 with a fanfare of trumpets the President and the Cardinal arrived, greeted me warmly, we took our seats on the platform, and breakfast was served. At each end of our table was a speaker's rostrum, one with the Vatican flag, the other with the Philippino national flag.

After the main course had been served, the Justice Minister went to the Philippino rostrum and read a very long introduction, almost word for word my full Curriculum Vitae, which he had earlier asked me to send. During the warm applause that followed I took my place at the Vatican rostrum and began my address. The previous year's speaker had been Mother Teresa and the year before that had been an American Presidential candidate, so I was in good company! The topic I had been asked to address was about young people in the world-wide Catholic Church, and I had prayed and worked hard to put together a challenging thirty minute talk, which was extremely well received and applauded at length. The President then went to the other rostrum and spent seven minutes thanking me very warmly. Breakfast finished, and we mingled with the guests for almost an hour, receiving a lot of very positive comments. I had noticed that interestingly everyone was wearing dark suits – I was the only person in a formal Philippino shirt!

Avoiding the Pope?

Sue and I were due to fly to Singapore early in the afternoon on the first leg of our journey home, and Pope St. John Paul II was due to arrive at the airport at lunchtime for an official visit. So the President offered us a lift to the airport with him, as he, of course, was going to meet the Pope. So we brought down our luggage, and I had changed into my suit – only to discover that everyone else had changed into their formal Philippino shirts! Our flight took off shortly after the Pope landed, so we saw him disembark and kiss the ground, as he was greeted by the Presidential party. When I saw him in Rome a few weeks later, he said he had heard that I delivered a very fine talk at the Prayer Breakfast in Manila, and then smiling he enquired why we had to leave, just as he was arriving?!

Pentecost 1998 in Rome

For the eve of Pentecost 1998, Pope St. John Paul II had issued an open invitation to all the worldwide Catholic Charismatic Renewal and all the New Catholic Movements in the Church to meet him in St. Peter's Square. Almost half a million people gathered, and following an amazing time of praise in a variety of languages, a tour of the whole area by the Pope in his Popemobile, the founders of four key Movements – the Focolare, the Neocatechumenal Way, L'Arche and Communion and Liberation – all gave a short presentation of their vision and ministry, after which the Pope gave a really encouraging address which brought together Scripture and Vatican II teaching:

The Spirit is always awesome whenever He intervenes. He arouses astonishing new events; He radically changes people and history. This was the unforgettable experience of the Second Vatican Council, during which, guided by the same Spirit, the Church rediscovered the charismatic dimension as essential to her identity.

He clearly saw the charismatic dimension as an essential part of the life of the Church, and went on to speak specifically of the charisms:

Today, to all of you gathered here in St. Peter's Square and to all Christians, I want to cry out: be open and docile to the gifts of the Spirit! Accept with gratitude and obedience the charisms that the Spirit never ceases to bestow! Do not forget that each charism is given for the common good, that is, for the benefit of the whole Church!

His final words were an impassioned prayer:

Come Holy Spirit and make the charisms you have bestowed ever more fruitful! Give new strength and missionary zeal to these sons and daughters of yours who are gathered here. Enlarge their hearts, enliven their Christian commitment in the world! Make them courageous messengers of the Gospel, witnesses of the risen Jesus Christ.

MY RESPONSE

Because the Catholic Charismatic Renewal is not a Movement as such – it has no human founder and no official membership – I was asked to respond to the words of the Pope on behalf of the CCR rather than to speak before him with the four Movement founders. So in my response I thanked him for inviting us to meet him publicly at St. Peter's Square at Pentecost, and for his clear, direct and very encouraging endorsement of the work of the Spirit in bringing us into being after Vatican II, and for his specific endorsement of the importance of the charismatic gifts in the Church, which he clearly saw as an essential part of her life. I must say that responding to a Papal address in St. Peter's Square in Rome in front of half a million people, with an unseen international television audience, was a very definite reminder to me of how far the Lord had brought me personally in the twenty two years since my baptism in the Holy Spirit. To emphasise this even more, I heard from an old school friend who had seen me on the national news in Brazil, and wanted to know what had happened to me, as his Stonyhurst memories were not of a particularly 'religious' friend!

UNEXPECTED ECUMENISM IN JOHANNESBURG

On another occasion I was going to Johannesburg, South Africa, to speak at a big conference with several bishops present, when I heard that the centre where the meeting was going to be held had been damaged by fire and could not be used. To everyone's amazement a large Protestant Church offered the use of their very fine, newly built church, with a magnificent large audience hall. As a church they never spoke English, everything was in Afrikaans, and none of the local black people were allowed to be members or even to enter the

building, whilst of course our Catholic Charismatic
Conference was fifty percent black! It turned out to be a
memorable event. The Pastor welcomed us including all our
black participants very warmly, his people served
refreshments, and as the Sunday closing day of the Conference
approached, he proposed a joint communion service. The
Catholic bishops who were present worked out a way that the
Pastor and one of them would both preach, the bread and wine
would be consecrated on two separate tables, and would then
be passed down the rows of the big mixed congregation,
to be either received or prayerfully passed on. It was
unconventional, but a ground-breaking moment which gave
rise to a committed search for greater unity. Throughout our
week, members of the Protestant Church had occupied the top
circle in the big hall to enjoy the worship and to watch the
black Africans praising God in song and dance. An amusing
thing for me was that before my first talk an elderly Irish priest
carrying a violin, came to tell me that a couple of times during
my scheduled sixty minute talk he would stand up and give
me a sign. I should finish my sentence and then leave the
microphone so that he could come up and play his fiddle. The
black Africans would dance all around the hall for a few
minutes and then I would continue my talk. Everyone loved
these occasional intermissions which happened about twice
during each of my talks. The watching Protestants saw these
as the highlights of the sessions!

During the conference I was staying with a charming couple
who were key local leaders, and after collecting me at the

airport they took me to their home. We entered a very well protected area of housing for white South Africans, where the houses we drove past all had walls topped with barbed wire and double entrance gates, until we reached a nice bungalow which had none of this protection. They told me I would be perfectly secure in my ground floor bedroom and must not be worried – they did so much with the local black township, helping them in so many ways, that nobody would ever think of breaking into their bungalow! I knew this was true, and slept very peacefully every night.

VISITS TO INDIA

As ICCRS President, I made two visits to India - both remarkable for a variety of reasons. As my British Airways flight approached Bombay/Mumbai on my first visit, the captain announced that unfortunately we would not be allowed to leave the airport as a curfew was in force, as apparently some Muslims had desecrated a Hindu shrine. An open conflict had broken out between the two groups, who were now fighting and killing each other on the streets. So the army had been brought in to restore order, and their first step had been to ban everyone except medical and religious leaders from the streets. We duly landed, passed through immigration control, but were detained with our luggage in the arrivals area. Much to my surprise, an airport official was walking among us asking for Mr. Charles Whitehead. So I was taken through to the general airport area to be greeted by Fr. Rufus Pereira in the biggest dog-collar I had ever seen, with an Indian lady who garlanded me with an enormous bouquet of flowers, much to the amazement of my fellow passengers. I was escorted out to a waiting chauffeur-driven limousine – an old American black Buick with more chromium plate than paintwork and an enormous crucifix with a statue of Our Lady on the dashboard! Fr. Rufus was making it clear that he was a religious leader and therefore entitled to be out and about! Ours was the only car on the road as we left the airport and proceeded towards the city at a speed of 20 miles per hour - apparently our impressive limousine only had first and second gears in working order! As we made our way towards the city, we passed groups of Indian military on patrol, saw buildings everywhere that were on fire, and heard the sound of constant rifle shots with the occasional machine gun. Most of the events at which I was to speak on the first two days had been cancelled by the military, but then order was restored and the curfew was lifted.

The lady who had garlanded me at the airport turned out to be my travelling companion during my time in India. She lived in England but often returned home, and her main responsibility was to check whatever food was served to me, where and how it had been prepared, before I was allowed to eat it. On a number of occasions she told me not to touch what had been put before me – very tricky when my hosts had prepared the food – but very helpful too, as in three weeks I was never once ill.

A CONFERENCE WITH MOTHER TERESA
Another lasting memory is from my second trip to India to

speak at their National Conference in Madras. I was told that about 25,000 people would attend, and the other main speaker was Mother Teresa, who would be coming just for the morning of the third day. She was expected the previous afternoon but telephoned to say she had so much to do in Calcutta that she would travel the following morning. This would cause chaos for the organisers, who had arranged massive security to cope with the extra 10,000 people who would come to welcome her on her arrival as well as to hear her speak the following morning. After much animated discussion an official from Air India organised an unofficial 'delay' to the last afternoon flight from Calcutta so that Mother could catch it. Apparently it was often late anyway!

THAT HESSION SACK

The following morning I was seated on the platform with the Archbishop of Madras, between Mother Teresa and one of her Sisters. I noticed that the Sister had brought with her a large hession sack, and when I asked her about this she replied that all would be clear shortly. Mother spoke about God's love for us all with wonderful simplicity, the Archbishop thanked her profusely and presented her with a beautiful silver cross which she passed to her companion. It went straight into the hession sack. As we left the platform we were protected by strong lines of security guards, but still members of the now 35,000 strong crowd managed to pass lots of things to Mother, ranging from family photos, written prayer requests, to all sorts of gifts and spiritual memorabilia. Mother thanked each of the donors by joining her hands and bowing her head, and everything went into the sack. Before we reached the exit the sack was so full that I had to help Sister to carry it. We reached our car and I sat in the back with Mother and Sister, with a security man in the front. We set off pursued by a determined crowd, some of whom were on the car bonnet and the roof. When I asked what would happen to them I was told the driver would deal with them. This he duly did at the first corner, where he accelerated before braking hard, at which everyone went flying off the car! I was assured everyone was expecting this and no-one would be hurt. Sister told me that in the evening Mother would take the contents of the sack into their chapel where she would pray for the person associated with every single item. After that all the cards and requests would be placed at the altar, while all the other things, including the Archbishop's silver cross, would be sold and the money put into Mother's work with the poor and the sick. I had the privilege of meeting Mother Teresa three times over the years, and she always remembered me and had the time for a short conversation and a prayer. Just as with Pope John Paul II, when I think back I realise how blessed I was to share in prayer on more than one occasion with Mother Teresa also.

MY NOBLE SHEET

When my friend John Noble heard that I was going to India the first time, he advised me to take a thin cotton sheet, sewn up into a tube, with a big flap to go over my head. This was to deal with mosquitoes during the night. I took his advice but thought little of it, until one night I was staying in a room with a window that would not close. My host family advised me to turn the ceiling fan onto full power as this would keep any mosquitoes out. Unfortunately the noise made by the fan was like Concorde taking off, so I resorted to John Noble's special sheet. All night long I could hear large numbers of mosquitoes all around me, but I enjoyed a peaceful night's sleep without suffering from a single bite – another reason to be grateful to my friend John Noble! When I woke up the next morning and went into the bathroom, I was surprised to see a snake relaxing in the water in the lavatory bowl. Travelling overseas usually has a few memorable moments!

OTHER ICCRS EVENTS
There were many other ICCRS and personal events during my Presidency, as I spoke at gatherings all over the world (the USA, Australia, Canada, all over Asia, Eastern and Western Europe, Latin America, Hong Kong, Japan, Jamaica, Pakistan, Singapore, Africa, South Korea and more) but those I have described were particularly memorable for obvious reasons. After each ICCRS conference or retreat in Italy, we usually had a meeting of all the delegates with Pope John Paul II, at which I would make a speech presenting us to him and outlining what we had been doing at our event. His responses always conveyed his personal endorsement of the CCR and the work of ICCRS, and in between these events we often had a private Council meeting with him as already explained. This gave us the opportunity to keep him up to date with what was happening in the world-wide Renewal, and to ask his advice and support when needed. There was never any doubt of his personal and official support for our work.

Papal Support

In the same way, my successors as ICCRS President, Alan
Panozza, Michelle Moran and Jim Murphy, enjoyed the
support of Popes Benedict and Francis. Benedict still always
describes himself as *'a friend of the Catholic Charismatic Renewal'*
and this dates back to the very early days when Cardinal
Suenens was looking into the authenticity of the CCR and had
enlisted the help and advice of a young German theologian,
Fr. Ratzinger. Sue and I have actively promoted ecumenical
relations in the world-wide Charismatic Renewal, particularly
after my ICCRS Presidency when I had more time available,
and I will write more about this in the next chapter. This area
of ministry has enjoyed full Papal support too, and been
greatly facilitated by the fact that I had established a good level
of credibility with the Catholic hierarchy during my time in
Rome.

A Trip to Buenos Aires to meet a future Pope

In 2005, Sue and I took a small group of Pentecostal and
Evangelical leaders from ICC, some with their wives, to
Buenos Aires, Argentina, to meet Cardinal Bergolio. Kevin and
Dorothy Ranaghan came with us, along with our Swedish
Lutheran friend Carl-Gustav Stenback, Olaf Franke from
Berlin, Vinson Synan and his wife from the USA, John Hall
from England, and Fran Armitage who was working closely
with us at ICCOWE (now ICC) and is still a wonderfully
committed and faithful friend in all our ICC work. We
were grateful that our trip was facilitated hugely by Nelly and
Jose-Luis Picone, key leaders in the CCR in Argentina. The

reason for the visit was that relations between Catholics and Pentecostals in the Latin American countries were often strained, and the main exception to this was in Buenos Aires where Cardinal Bergoglio had built strong, friendly and co-operative relationships with the local Pentecostals, and we were hoping his advice would be helpful for other areas.

A FUTURE POPE

The Cardinal met us at his home/offices on a Saturday morning, and we discovered he had invited YWAM - Youth With A Mission - to use his top floor as their office, a clear sign of his willingness to co-operate with groups that were not Catholic. He told us that the key to working together was simple – establish close personal friendships with the local Pentecostal and Evangelical pastors, pray, share and have meals together, take part in one another's gatherings, and go out on the streets to evangelise. Often he had decided to make the first move and in his experience he had always received a warm welcome. Before we left him, Cardinal Bergoglio knelt down in front of us and asked that we pray over him for more of the Holy Spirit, *'particularly the ladies'* he said *'because women's prayers are always very powerful'*. So Sue and others laid hands on him and we all prayed over him for several minutes. Later that day one of our Pentecostal brothers told us that as we had prayed, he had a word from the Lord that this man was to be a future Pope. Here again, what a privilege to lay hands in prayer on the future Pope Francis!

A Remarkable Man

As we were leaving him, he came out carrying a large bag of pasta to catch a bus into the heart of the city, where he was going to cook a meal for some of the poorest residents. When we later met a number of the city's Pentecostal pastors, they all expressed great admiration and affection for Bergoglio, with whom they prayed regularly, and took part in each other's meetings and church events. It was clear that a strong bond had been established among them – an example to us all. So you can imagine how excited we were when he was elected Pope, bringing to this highest office a practical commitment to Christian unity and a very positive personal experience of relationships with the Pentecostals and New Charismatic Church leaders in particular. This has stayed with him and he has continued to build personal friendships with an increasing number of them, meeting both publicly and privately, and often inviting them to have a meal with him. With great delight they often send me emails of official photographs taken when they were meeting him or enjoying a meal together! When I was to be introduced to him in 2014 at a big gathering in Rome, he stepped forward to embrace me with the words, *'I remember you – you came to talk to me about Pentecostals a few years ago!'* In my view he is exactly the person the Catholic Church needs at this time. Some who are opposed to change try to undermine him, but he has a clear vision of where the Church needs to be changing and moving forward, and he will not be side-tracked from this. A truly remarkable and anointed man.

TWELVE

THE INTERNATIONAL CHARISMATIC CONSULTATION ON WORLD EVANGELISATION (ICCOWE)

M Y JOURNEY INTO A LIVING FAITH and Sue's conversion from atheism both owed so much to members of other Christian Churches, not Catholics, that it was very natural for us to become involved in building ecumenical contacts and promoting relationships with Christian brothers and sisters from other traditions. This area of interest had brought me into contact with **Canon Michael Harper**, a key Anglican figure in the Charismatic Renewal who had established The Fountain Trust, SOMA, Renewal Magazine, and the Charismatic Leaders Conference, among many other things. In 1983 he invited me to join the Charismatic Leaders Conference, and I have written about this annual event in another chapter.

THE SINGAPORE CONSULTATIONS

In 1987 I received an invitation from Michael to attend the Singapore Consultation – an international gathering of significant charismatic leaders from all Christian traditions who would meet in a hotel in Singapore to decide how we might co-operate in international evangelisation. There were in fact two Singapore gatherings in successive years, both addressed by top speakers from Catholic, Protestant, Pentecostal and New Churches, and Michael established a committee consisting of himself, Fr. Tom Forrest and Reverend Larry Christenson to move things forward with the full backing of nearly all the attendees at the two Consultations. It was at the Singapore Consultations that I first got to know Fr. Raniero Cantalamessa, the official Preacher to the Papal Household of John Paul II, and also where I received a prophetic word when I was travelling up to my room in the hotel lift, telling me that I was to be a future President of the International Catholic Charismatic Renewal Council, of which I was not even a member at the time! Just in case I had any doubts about this, an Italian lady gave me the same prophetic word the following day.

The name chosen for the new ecumenical organisation meeting for the Singapore Consultations was the International Charismatic Consultation on World Evangelisation, abbreviated to **ICCOWE**. Regional sub-committees were established around the world, and conferences were held to promote the ICCOWE vision of working closely together across the whole body of Christ to preach the Gospel and evangelise. Meetings were held in the USA, in Asia, and in Europe, several of which I was able to attend.

INTERNATIONAL ECUMENICAL GATHERINGS
The most significant of these gatherings was in Brighton in 1991, for which I was a local committee member, and which included sessions led by the Archbishop of Canterbury, George Carey, and by Cardinal Basil Hume, the Archbishop of Westminster. The Papal Preacher, Fr. Raniero Cantalamessa

gave a keynote address, and this event gave birth to a widespread interest in ecumenical initiatives, accompanied by a considerable amount of press interest, positive publicity and new activities. Brighton was followed by two gatherings in Prague and several others around the world. At the second Prague Conference in the year 2000, Michael Harper stepped down as Chairman of ICCOWE, and as I was now no longer Chairman of the International Catholic Charismatic Renewal Council I was elected in his place.

CHAIRMAN OF **ICCOWE**

My first conference as chairman took place in **Malta** in 2004 under the title of 'The Suffering Church'. I had initially wanted to call it 'The Persecuted Church' but was advised that this would make attendance by some countries very difficult. We decided to have a special stream within the programme for theologians, in which they would meet for one session each day. After the Conference was over, we published the theological papers as a book, entitled 'The Suffering Body – Responding to the Persecution of Christians', edited by Harold H. Hunter and Cecil M. Robeck, published by Paternoster in 2006. The main general participants included some who had experienced persecution for their faith, together with a number of politicians, including our friend Lord Alton, who were known to campaign actively for total freedom for people to practise their faith wherever they were. I was particularly delighted that we attracted a good number of key leaders from every expression of the body of Christ, including some well-known Pentecostals and New Charismatic Church leaders.

The Vatican sent several of their experts, and the general level of experience and involvement in the suffering present in the world-wide church was impressive. It was an excellent week and made a considerable contribution to an improved general understanding of the suffering and persecution experienced by members of all the denominations and fellowships.

THE INTERNATIONAL CHARISMATIC CONSULTATION - ICC
Although we did not anticipate this at the time, Malta turned out to be the most recent large international gathering organized by ICCOWE. With an increasing number of regional events taking place, there was less need for the big international conferences, the costs of which were becoming too high for many who would normally have participated. Michael Harper had set up a small team to facilitate the various gatherings and conferences, and the key team member was Fran Armitage, who has continued to serve ICCOWE over the years and is still actively doing so today by making possible the bi-annual 'Gatherings in the Holy Spirit' which take place in Rome for invited Catholic and New Independent Charismatic Church leaders. Fran has also maintained all the records of the ICCOWE events over the years, and has been able to place some of them in the Donald Gee Foundation archives, currently held at Mattersey Hall. ICCOWE has now been abbreviated to **ICC**, the International Charismatic Consultation, which continues to encourage contacts and relationships within a wide area of the body of Christ. This on-going contribution made by ICC to the growing unity in the Christian world, particularly with some of the less

structured charismatic fellowships, remains extremely valuable and should never be overlooked or discounted. Sue and I will always be committed to this vital work of the Holy Spirit, as will our dear friend Fran who, with the backing of her husband Godfrey, was with us when we went to Buenos Aires to see Cardinal Bergoglio.

THIRTEEN

GATHERINGS IN THE HOLY SPIRIT

I N THE LATE 1980S AND THE EARLY 1990S, the European Catholic Charismatic leaders had held meetings to bring some of the national Catholic leaders together and there had also been gatherings to include leaders from other parts of the body of Christ. These had all been very helpful in building relationships and encouraging co-operation in a variety of ways. Kim Kollins, a Catholic leader from America who was resident in Germany and had become a member of the Beatitudes Community, was very active in these gatherings. She had also become aware that the Vatican Pontifical Council for Promoting Christian Unity had established extensive contacts across the main Protestant denominations as well as with some Pentecostals, but had not found a way of relating to the New Independent Charismatic Churches. The main reason for this was that these churches did not have any central body to represent them, but really were independent – as their name suggests. They were, however, probably the fastest growing part of Western Christianity.

A VISION BECOMES REALITY

So with the support of Fr. Jim Puglisi from the Rome-based Centro pro Unione, and Reverend Peter Dippl, a Berlin-based Pentecostal Pastor, she approached the Unity Council and proposed setting up some gatherings in the Holy Spirit to which key leaders of the New Independent Charismatic Churches and of the International Catholic Charismatic Renewal would be invited. A small group, of which I was a member, was brought together to take things forward with the support of the Unity Council, and it was decided to hold 'Gatherings in the Holy Spirit' in Rome to make the vision a reality. This duly happened, and to date there have been nine meetings in Rome in alternate years, consisting of about 60-70 leaders each time. For the last six meetings I have served as the Catholic co-chair of the organising committee, and the planned 2020 meeting will be our tenth.

A KEY DOCUMENT

The 'Gatherings in the Holy Spirit' have been one of the most rewarding and personally satisfying areas of my ministry, and have to a large extent fulfilled the original vision of establishing contact between the Council for Unity and the New Independent Church leaders. An additional annual meeting has been held for the last six years, at which five leaders of the New Independent Charismatic Churches have spent one or two days with a team of five from the Council for Unity to develop their mutual understanding and relationships. I serve as a member of the Council for Unity's team; our times together include lunches and dinners, and we produce an internal report on our discussions. Mutual understanding and appreciation has blossomed, and the first public fruit of our sessions is the production of a document written by Richard Roberts, one of the Independent group, at the request of the Council for Unity, which describes and explains the New Charismatic Churches - what they are, how they operate, their aims and mission etc. It has been studied and revised with the advice of many of their key leaders around the world, and the work of drafting and co-ordinating has been undertaken by Richard Roberts, who is a committee member for the 'Gatherings' and a member of the team in dialogue with the Council for Unity. It has now been 'signed off' and the Council for Unity have published it on their web-site. It's hard to over-estimate the significance of this publication – absolutely the first of its kind from these impressive New Churches, who today are one of the fastest growing Christian groups. A copy of Richard Roberts' paper entitled 'Characteristics of the New Charismatic Churches' may be obtained on-line at the Pontifical Council for Christian Unity's web-site. Where we go from here has yet to be decided, but this on its own has made the 'Gatherings in the Holy Spirit' well worth all the effort poured into them. There have, of course, been amazing friendships and relationships established, leading to co-operation and working together in numerous ways. The Lord certainly blesses His people when we make the effort to come together across traditional boundaries, and much of Kim Kollins' prophetic vision is being fulfilled.

AN INSPIRATION!
I have been so blessed to be part of all this, and our bi-annual Gatherings in Rome never fail to inspire, inform, encourage and support all who participate, whether Catholic or Independent leaders. When I add in the conversations taking place with the Pontifical Council for the Promotion of

Christian Unity I see the Holy Spirit at work in a remarkable way, and the original vision being wonderfully realised. In my own personal walk with the Lord I have been enormously inspired and encouraged by a number of New Charismatic Church leaders like John Wimber, and I briefly refer to this in chapter 18.

As Pope Francis points out in his letter to the Church, *'Evangelii Gaudium – the Joy of the Gospel' sections 244-246:*

> *'If we really believe in the abundantly free working of the Holy Spirit, we can learn so much from one another! It is not just about being better informed about others, but rather about reaping what the Spirit has sown in them, which is also meant to be a gift for us. Through an exchange of gifts, the Spirit can lead us ever more fully into truth and goodness'.*

This has certainly been my experience since I opened my life to the presence and the work of the Holy Spirit in 1976.

Sue and Charles with Pope Francis at Pentecost 2019

FOURTEEN

CHARISMATICS AND PENTECOSTALS TOGETHER

W HEN I BECAME A MEMBER of the English National
Service Committee in 1982, I also received an
invitation to join the **'Charismatic Leaders
Conference'**, which had been founded by Canon Michael
Harper in the 1970s. It consisted of people who were seen as
key charismatic leaders in the mainline denominations, the
Pentecostals, and the New Charismatic Churches. When I
was invited to join, the only other active Catholic member was
Fr. Ian Petit OSB. Bob Balkam (NSC Chairman) and Bishop
Ambrose Griffiths OSB had attended but not regularly. The
Conference met annually, moving between different venues
around the country, and it seemed to me that Catholic
members were looked upon with interest and curiosity.
Fr. Ian was accepted as a very wise and spiritual man, but a
youngish (I was 39) Catholic married layman was a novelty!

A VERY SPECIAL SMALL GROUP

In my first couple of years as a member, a number of the
Independent and Pentecostal leaders tried in subtle
conversations to show me the error of my ways, suggesting
that I would be more comfortable joining them. My room-mate
at my first meeting spent a couple of hours pointing out all
that his fellowship could offer me, until I eventually fell asleep!
I had become accustomed to a charismatic person being
something of an oddity among my 'normal' fellow Catholics,

but it came as a surprise that a charismatic Catholic needed to see the error of his ways among some of the Pentecostal and Independent leaders. But I very much enjoyed the meetings – the praise and worship was amazing, the talks were excellent, and the fellowship and informal discussions were fascinating. In my first year we had a couple of sessions in small groups for sharing, prayer and ministry, which were put together alphabetically. My group members were Arthur Wallis, David Watson, Colin Urquhart, Terry Virgo and David Wilkinson – five of the most powerful, influential and innovative leaders attending the event! So I committed myself to attending every year.

A New Chairman

As the founder, Michael Harper was chairman, but in my second year it was decided to hold an election for a new chairman in order to ensure that there was variety and change after ten years. As we prayed and discerned, there were prophetic words, for example *'the axe is laid to the root of the tree'*, and I began to realise that many of the members were looking for change. So I was not surprised when John Noble, a New Charismatic Church leader, was elected the new chairman. I had already formed a very positive view of John who had welcomed me very warmly, accepting me for who I was, and going out of his way to make me feel at home, so I had in fact voted for him. Over the next few years I found I became fully accepted by everyone and the slight negativity about Catholicism disappeared. In fact John Noble approached me with Gerald Coates, to offer to help me develop my leadership skills by going as a guest to their Pioneer Leaders Conferences. They recognised that there were hardly any UK examples of Catholic lay leaders from whom I could learn, and so with the promise that they had no desire to 'convert' me, they helped me greatly at several of their conferences and prayed for me constantly. I owe them a great debt of gratitude as I really learned an enormous amount from them. John in particular has been a good friend ever since, and is currently a Trustee of ICC and a Committee Member for the 'Gatherings in the Holy Spirit'.

CO-CHAIRMAN WITH HUGH OSGOOD
As the years passed I found I was more and more accepted by the Protestant, Independent and Pentecostal leaders, but it still came as a surprise when in 2003 John Noble approached me to say he was stepping down as chairman and wondered how I might feel about taking on this responsibility, perhaps along with someone else. Thus it transpired that my Pentecostal friend, Hugh Osgood, and I were elected as joint chairmen of the conference when John stepped down. My wife Sue took on the role of secretary, with the help of Hugh's administrative team. My journey as a member of the conference has been an interesting one, from the 'novelty' Catholic member who probably needed to see the error of his ways, to the respected and valued co-chairman with my well-known brother Hugh, who is currently one of the Presidents of Churches Together in England and Wales. I think my journey illustrated the massive work of the Holy Spirit to build unity from all sides, making it clear that this renewal movement across the whole

body of Christ had the building of close relationships as a key objective. In the 1980s and 90s there were many in all expressions of Christianity who had not yet seen this, but today, thanks to the commitment to unity of more and more of our leaders at every level, the visible expressions of our relationships in Christ are transforming our churches and fellowships. Long may it continue!

ATTRACTING YOUNGER LEADERS

Today this leaders' conference is known as 'The Charismatic and Pentecostal Leaders' Conference', and Hugh and I with our small leadership team, are looking at ways of attracting younger leaders to join the conference. Our efforts are bearing fruit, and we are seeing a variety of young leaders working with us. The main way this is coming about is by inviting them to plan part of the content of the next conference with us; their contributions are excellent and we are seeing increasing interest from more of our younger leaders across the full spectrum of churches. We see this as absolutely essential for our future, and we are rightly remaining fully charismatic in all that we do. The alternative – which is not uncommon – is to just 'keep the show on the road' as the participants become older, and we become the past leaders of this Charismatic and Pentecostal experience. This may lead to an easier life but it is a recipe for disappearance – something we are not willing to accept, no matter what challenges we may have to face. Exciting for me is that we have attracted several young Catholic leaders who are playing an active part in this move forward.

ALWAYS SOMETHING NEW

The Christian journey is supposed to be an exciting one with new challenges facing us all the time, no matter how young or old we may be. If this is not our experience, then something is wrong, and we need to seriously examine before the Lord where we are and what we're doing. For me, three priorities are always:

-   Baptism in the Holy Spirit for everyone
-   Building unity based on relationships throughout the body of Christ
-   Training young leaders and releasing them into ministry.

I have always felt called to promote these three areas as part of whatever I am doing. Great things unfold as a result of following our calling, things beyond our expectations. One thing is certain – these great things will be for the expansion of God's reign, a reign of love, justice and peace. Every calling is intended to bring this about.

THREE AREAS OF ECUMENICAL MISSION

In my ecumenical work, I am privileged to be a Trustee of the Anglican 'Christian Healing Mission', which under the anointed leadership of Rev. John Ryeland and his wife Gillian ministers healing to those in need, and promotes Encounter Prayer in parishes and fellowships around the country. The London based Antioch Community, part of the Sword of the Spirit international group, is an ecumenical body providing spiritually for families and for those called to be single for the

Lord. Here I have been a Trustee for more than twenty years, but always feel I receive more than I give. I was also a Board member, and later a Trustee, for Premier Christian Radio in its early years, helping it become established as one of the world's foremost Christian broadcasters, serving all the churches and fellowships in the UK and beyond. I remain in close touch with the Director, Peter Kerridge, and I'm always available to give advice and help. These three areas of service have been and remain very important in my life, and are good examples of how there are always new challenges and changes to be faced as we follow the leading of the Spirit.

As I write this, the Christian Healing Mission is seeing its focus move from a staffed centre to which people come for ministry to a small team which takes the message of Encounter Prayer and Healing Ministry to local parishes, churches and fellowships. This has meant selling the fairly large premises from which the Mission has been operating, and reducing staff. The Holy Spirit is moving us on. The Antioch Community has moved a number of families out from its centre in Ealing, West London, to Hillingdon, where property is less expensive, and is establishing a new base there. Premier Christian Radio is planning to move its operating centre to an old Anglican Church built by Sir Christopher Wren on the edge of the City of London, where extensive internal re-structuring will be needed to accommodate its technical requirements whilst retaining an area for services and worship. The demands of the digital age also offer amazing new opportunities to extend its service and ministry into a wealth of new areas. Life in the Spirit never stands still – there is always more and we must be prepared to embrace change.

FGBMFI - The Full Gospel Business Men's Fellowship International
During the 1980s I was active in the **FGBMFI**, a remarkable Christian organisation founded in 1953 by Demos Shakarian and now present in 150 countries, whose members include every race, culture, social status and language. Their focus is to build relationships, particularly among men engaged in the world of work, in order to preach the Gospel and extend God's Kingdom. They do this by calling people back to God, promoting integrity and good character, impacting our leaders and culture, and by taking the message of God's love to every family. Their aim is to help people find a better life by lifting up Christ in every business centre, every marketplace, every government centre, and every university in every nation, city and town in the world.

Members meet in local Chapters and gather together Christians from across the churches and fellowships to pray together and to organise area dinners. To these they invite non-Christian friends and colleagues to listen to an invited speaker sharing testimony and presenting the basic Gospel message in a straightforward way, followed by the offer of prayer for those who wish to respond. During my own years of active involvement, I set up a Chapter in my local area which put on regular dinners, and I also travelled to speak at dinners in various parts of the country. It was a fruitful time during which I saw a significant number of people come to faith and give their lives to the Lord. But when I became the President of ICCRS, as recounted in chapter 10, I could no longer commit the necessary time to leading a Chapter, and so I passed this responsibility over to others. I still speak from time to time at a dinner, and I'm always reminded of what an effective way this is to reach men in particular, in business and the professions with the Gospel message.

FIFTEEN

AZUSA STREET: 100 YEARS OF BLESSING

I N 2004, I RECEIVED A LETTER FROM THE CHAIRMAN of the Azusa Street Centennial Cabinet, inviting me to be the twelfth member of his Cabinet to help them plan the 2006 one hundredth anniversary of the beginning of Pentecostalism at the fellowship which met in Azusa Street, Los Angeles, in 1906. I was absolutely amazed, particularly as he said I would be the only non-Pentecostal leader in the Cabinet, and so would be representing the rest of world Christianity! We had met when he came to our ICC Conference on 'The Suffering Church' in Malta in 2004, and he was very supportive of the vision and work of ICC. The Cabinet would pay for me to travel to Los Angeles every two months for a Cabinet meeting lasting three days, and would accommodate me in the hotel of the meeting. The event we would be planning and leading would be a seven day gathering in Los Angeles in April 2006, at which Pentecostal leaders from all over the world would be invited to celebrate their first 100 years. About 70,000 were expected to attend.

100 YEARS OF PENTECOSTALISM
The Centennial would be in celebration of what happened in April 1906 when a young evangelical pastor, William J. Seymour, was asked to leave the church he was pastoring because of his focus on the gifts of the Holy Spirit, and he could only find a vacancy at the small, very poor, ethnically

diverse church in Azusa Street, Los Angeles, where they were willing to accept him as their pastor. So that is where he went. He again taught about the charismatic gifts of the Spirit *(1 Corinthians 12)* and the congregation experienced remarkable outpourings of the Holy Spirit at their services, with manifestations of the gifts of tongues, prophecy, miracles and healings. The word spread, and evangelicals from a wide area began to come to Azusa Street to experience the power of the Spirit for themselves. Then returning to their own churches full of the Spirit, they began to minister this grace to their fellow members, only to find they were often asked to stop doing this. Unable to deny what they had experienced, many of them left their churches and began to meet in fellowship with others who shared their experience of the power of the Spirit. These new fellowships grew rapidly in numbers, spreading widely, and became known as Pentecostals. Very soon they were the fastest growing part of world-wide Christianity and had spread to every country. This is what was to be celebrated in 2006 in Los Angeles, at the Azusa Street Centennial, the 100th anniversary of the birth of Pentecostalism.

ENDORSEMENT FROM ROME

I felt honoured to receive their invitation to join the Centennial Cabinet of 12, but before accepting I contacted the Pontifical Council for the Promotion of Christian Unity, and travelled to Rome to meet Cardinal Walter Kasper. I did this because I did not want to cause problems in the work for unity in California, or with the American Catholic Bishops Conference, so I asked

the Cardinal for his advice. He echoed my own feelings that
to receive such an invitation was a great honour and an
amazing privilege that they would invite a Catholic to join
their Cabinet. After spending a couple of hours with him on a
Saturday morning talking about relationships between
Catholics and Pentecostals around the world, he told me
that in his view I absolutely must accept their invitation.
He assured me that he would personally talk to the Cardinal
in Los Angeles to head off any possible difficulties and
misunderstandings. So I was delighted to accept the invitation
to join the Centennial Cabinet, also knowing I was doing so
with the blessing of the appropriate Vatican department.

THE CENTENNIAL CABINET

I attended my first Cabinet meeting a little nervously, but
received a very warm welcome from the other eleven
members, two or three of whom I had met before, but all of
whom were internationally known Pentecostal leaders. We
gathered in a very smart meeting room around a large table,
where we found our places indicated by a leather folder
bearing our names in gold letters. After praise, worship and
prayer, the background and vision for the event were
presented, and the document proposed for the first publicity
was given to us. It was impressive and attractively presented,
but when we went through the text there was one sentence
that caused me concern. In writing about baptism in the Holy
Spirit, the phrase *'with the only acceptable evidence of speaking in
tongues'* appeared. Now I knew that this view was held by
classical Pentecostals but it was not held by Catholic, Orthodox

and Protestant Charismatics, nor by some Pentecostals or the New Independent Charismatic Churches and Fellowships. So to include it as a key phrase in presenting the Azusa Street Centennial vision would not be helpful. I voiced my concerns which were greeted with total silence. Eventually one of my fellow Cabinet members spoke, agreeing that what I had said was of course correct, and that if we used this phrase about *'the only acceptable evidence'* we risked alienating a large part of the worldwide church, including a lot of Pentecostals. Others agreed, and pointed out that we did not need to include these few words. Hesitantly and with some reluctance, the Cabinet accepted what I had said, and I was thanked for my willingness to bring the subject up. From that moment onwards I became aware that attitudes towards me warmed, and I was accepted as a valued member of the Council and a real brother in Christ.

PERSONAL TESTIMONY!
I attended about eight such meetings as we prepared for the big event and I got to know my fellow Councillors well. Sue was invited to come with me to one of our preparatory gatherings. The Councillors ranged from strong itinerant exponents of the Prosperity Gospel and well-known TV personalities, to pastors of enormous churches in Africa and Asia – a real cross-section of worldwide Pentecostalism. When it came to the week-long Centennial celebrations in April 2006, to my great surprise I was asked to be an MC for part of the big opening session and to share my personal testimony! This I did and received a standing ovation from the

20,000 plus delegates gathered at our main venue, where the speaker that evening was Benny Hinn, whom I already knew. Because we numbered over 70,000 participants we were having to use four separate venues for our sessions, with the Cabinet members divided between them. Sue and I were always assigned to the main venue.

THE LORD AT WORK

The week passed far too quickly and was filled with amazing moments and inspiring speakers. At one session Council members, their wives, and some key speakers formed a line, and we prayed over several hundred young leaders who passed slowly in front of us. On another occasion we had an overflow of about 5,000 people at our main venue who were re-directed to the nearby sports stadium, so about twenty five of us went there to pray for them. Our leader told us not to talk to them when they came forward as it would take too long, but simply to lay hands on them and to pray for them in tongues for about thirty seconds. The Lord would do the rest! He then invited all 5,000 of them to come for prayer, forming lines in front of us to receive their thirty seconds of ministry without any conversation. The majority rested in the power of the Spirit, having said nothing more than their names. It took time, but when I had a chance afterwards to speak to some for whom I had prayed in tongues for the allotted thirty seconds, I was thrilled to hear of healings and special answers to prayer they had experienced. The lesson I learned was that God will work whatever the circumstances, and we must be careful not to make things too complicated.

An Amazing Week

During the week we had arranged for doctors, dentists and nurses to go in specially equipped vans to the large number of the poor and homeless of Los Angeles, who inhabited the streets in one particular area of the city, to offer medical attention, food, bedding and clothing according to their needs, and of course for prayer ministry to be offered as well. Short pilgrimages were available for participants in the conference to go to the site of the original Azusa Street chapel, now commemorated by a plaque in the beautiful grounds of the Japanese Centre, and there were wide choices of meetings and seminars every day in addition to the main sessions. 2006 seems a long time ago now, but we have many happy memories of that amazing week, attended by more than 70,000 Pentecostals from all over the world. What a privilege it was to be a Cabinet member!

Eleven Years Later

In Rome in 2017, when we gathered at Pentecost to celebrate fifty years of the Catholic Charismatic Renewal, it was a great joy to meet again some members of the Azusa Street Centennial Cabinet at a special meeting with Pope Francis on Pentecost eve morning, and then to sit with them behind him on the platform at Circus Maximus in the evening, in front of more than 50,000 Catholic Charismatics from around the world. It brought back many happy memories, and it was wonderful to listen to Pentecostal Pastor Giovanni Traettino and Fr. Raniero Cantalamessa, the two speakers invited to address us by Pope Francis in addition to himself, Patti

Mansfield of the Duquesne Weekend and Michelle Moran, ICCRS President.

THE ON-GOING WORK FOR UNITY

For us the Azusa Street Centennial was an extraordinary and wonderful occasion, and as I look back I can only marvel at the ground-breaking work of the Lord which made a Catholic charismatic layman play such an integral role in this amazing historic event. Alleluia! The Council for Laity in Rome and Cardinal Kasper at the Council for Unity had both requested that I visit them after our return home, as they were both very interested to know all that had happened in Los Angeles. They were delighted to hear of the part we had been asked to play in the centennial celebrations, and of the respect and honour with which we had been treated by the other Cabinet members. It was a source of great encouragement to us all in the work of building unity with the Pentecostal part of the body of Christ. Just a few weeks before I sat down to write this chapter, I received a telephone call from Pastor Billy Wilson who had chaired the Centennial Cabinet, to tell me that he and his wife were coming to London and inviting us to join them for lunch at their hotel. When we met, our relationships were just as strong as in 2006, and he was warmly encouraging us to join them as their guests at a big international gathering in Jerusalem the following year. The Lord is still working and building unity with this important part of His body, and tremendous progress has already been made, as we were reminded in 2017 at the Rome celebrations with Pope Francis of 50 years of the Catholic Charismatic Renewal. Alleluia!

SIXTEEN

CELEBRATE THE FAMILY

F ROM THE EARLY 1980s, SUE AND I WERE RESPONSIBLE with a small local team for organising and administering the annual Catholic Charismatic Conference at La Sainte Union College in Southampton. The Conference had been started in the late 1970s by a team made up mainly of local prayer group leaders, and I had been invited to join them in 1980. The team consisted of wonderfully committed people, and included Frances Weaver, Sr. Carmen Shields and Fr. Sean O'Haire. It has often been my experience that I quickly become chairman of such teams, and this happened following the unexpected illness of Fr. Sean. Sue later took on the main responsibility for administering the Conference, and Peter and Michelle Moran, founders of the Sion Community, joined the team.

THE SOUTHAMPTON CONFERENCE

It was a popular week-long residential event, with a workable capacity of up to 400 adults. The College facilities were good and we had the support of the resident community of La Sainte Union Sisters. The local leaders were hard-working and visionary, and we brought in excellent speakers from all over the world in addition to those who were UK based. We took a conscious decision to include charismatic speakers from other denominations and fellowships, which included pioneers like Anglican Reverends Michael Harper and Tom Smail, Baptist

Reverend Jim Graham and Independent Pastor David
Matthews. Among the well-known Catholic speakers were Fr.
Ian Petit OSB, Fr, Michael Simpson SJ, Fr. Bob Faricy from
Rome, Delia Smith, Fr. Ken Metz (ICCRO), Sr. Nancy Kellar,
Abbot Parry, Dom Benedict Heron, Frances Hogan and Fr. Bob
de Grandis. A very important part of the week, which always
produced excellent fruit in the participants lives, were the
small sharing groups which met several times. I personally
found them a great blessing.

THE LORD SPEAKS
In 1991, Sue and I felt the Lord was speaking to us about the
importance of a conference for families, the whole family,
including every age from babies upwards. At Southampton
we were limited by the College rules, which did not accept
young people under sixteen years of age for reasons of
insurance. We took the Lord's prompting seriously and waited
to see if it was confirmed in some way. It was, through
Scripture, with *Isaiah 54 verses 2 and 3 'enlarge the space of your
tents'*. We also had clear words from guest speakers, so in 1992
we invited about 30 of those involved with us to come together
for a weekend of prayer and discernment. They were so
positive about putting on a family conference that we took the
decision to go ahead immediately, even though this would
mean the closure of Southampton, which ended with a
weekend event in 1993.

A FAMILY CONFERENCE
We felt the way forward was to hold a week-long family

conference from Easter Sunday evening, as this would avoid clashing with any other established events, and would allow people to stay in their parishes until after Mass on Easter Sunday morning. The evangelical Protestant world was already running Spring Harvest at this time at the Butlins Holiday Camp in Minehead, under the leadership of Clive Calver. I knew Clive, so my first step was to talk to him about the possibility of including a Catholic stream which would have some separate sessions but share in most of the main conference. I was greatly encouraged in this by my good friend John Noble, a key leader in the New Charismatic Churches. Clive Calver responded enthusiastically, referring the suggestion to his trustees and financial backers. Sadly they turned down my request, much to Clive's regret. The time was just not right for this sort of unity with Catholics. Interestingly I was invited to speak at Spring Harvest in Minehead in 2017, twenty four years later, the first Catholic to receive such an invitation. It came through my good friend Malcolm Duncan, an Elim Pentecostal leader who spent seven years pastoring our local Baptist Church, Gold Hill, during which time we prayed together regularly and went on a two day retreat with the other local church leaders. Interestingly, Spring Harvest is now chaired by Duncan Calver, Clive's son. He couldn't wait to tell his father who their first Catholic speaker was. Things keep moving forward, if very slowly. In one session I shared the Spring Harvest platform with Archbishop Justin Welby, when we answered a wide range of questions on Christian unity in both serious and humorous ways, and received an extremely positive response from the big crowd who attended.

CELEBRATE!

So we embraced the challenge to go it alone with the family conference, which we decided to call CELEBRATE, and I wrote to every holiday camp in England and Wales to ask if they could accommodate a week-long Christian family conference, starting Easter Sunday afternoon. The main reason for looking at holiday camps as the venue was the self-catering accommodation many offered, as this would keep the costs down for families. In addition to family-friendly accommodation, we were looking for a large conference hall of some sort, and facilities to take streams of children and teenagers covering two academic years each for sessions every day – a total of eight groups in addition to the main adult conference.

'THE LORD HAS BEEN PROMPTING ME...'

By this stage we had developed a comprehensive vision for CELEBRATE, which is written out at the end of this chapter. We intended it to be an event which catered for every state of life and every age group from babies to the over eighties. It would begin with an evening celebration on Easter Sunday, the Wednesday would be a day off with an evening session, and we would end with lunch on the Saturday. So I sent off my letter to every Butlins, Pontins, Haven etc., more than 200 possible venues in all. As the replies started to come back we wondered if we were on the wrong track – none of them could accommodate us for a whole variety of different reasons.

Then a letter arrived from Clive Nottage, the General Manager of the John Fowler Holiday Park in Ilfracombe, Devon: **'Dear Charles, The Lord has been prompting me for two years to offer our Holiday Park for a Christian Conference at Easter, and I have just opened your letter.'**

When I telephoned Clive he told me he was a Reader at the local Anglican Church in Ilfracombe, and he suggested we visit the Holiday Park as soon as we could, so a few days later we were in Ilfracombe on the North Devon coast. The Holiday Park was perfect for our accommodation requirements, with self-catering chalet bungalows offering two to eight beds. Five hundred yards away was Ilfracombe College, a large secondary school which would provide all the facilities we needed for our main meeting hall and all the rooms for the young people and children's streams. Clive had already asked the head teacher about the possibility of renting the College to us, provided the school term dates allowed this, and had received a very positive response.

ACCEPTABLE SECURITY

Clive was happy for us to have exclusive use of the Holiday Park, which would take up to about 1,000 visitors, and of course this would be important for us as we doubted we could comfortably share the site with the regular Easter holidaymakers. If we needed alternative types of accommodation there were plenty of bed and breakfasts and small hotels in the town, and some people opted for these. We would of course have to cover the costs for the whole park even if the conference numbers fell below what would be needed, and

Clive had calculated that allowing for some discount we
would be looking at guaranteeing receipts for him of £46,000.
When we had finished the Southampton Conference a year
earlier our cash balance in the bank was £300, so to commit
ourselves to the John Fowler Holiday Park required a
considerable step of faith on all our parts! John Fowler himself,
the founder and owner of the group, was happy to welcome
us but quite reasonably required some security if he was only
accepting bookings from our conference people for one of his
busiest weeks in the year at his best site. The only security we
could offer was 'The Open House', our home in Gerrards
Cross, so in an exchange of letters he agreed that this was
acceptable as security, should the delegates fail to cover the
required £46,000. We never worried about this, simply because
we were sure that the Lord was at work in the whole initiative,
and when I look back I am so thankful He gave us the faith for
this and for all that has followed.

A NEW BEGINNING
So in Easter Week 1994 the first CELEBRATE Family
Conference happened in Ilfracombe, Devon, led by a team
from Catholic Charismatic Renewal but open to Christians
from all other traditions. We budgeted conservatively for 750
participants, and the Lord blessed us with over 900! The week
proved to be a great success in spite of some very bad weather,
and until 2015 we ran every year but one, and after the first
year our numbers were between 1,430 and our absolute
capacity of 1,500 in total, about 45% of whom were always
under the age of 25 years. What caused us to miss a year was

the fact that local Education Authorities were permitted to decide on the term dates in their areas, so when Easter was very late it was possible for them to have all the holidays before Easter Weekend and to open the schools again on Easter Tuesday. When this happened, we felt we could not hold the Conference before Easter in Lent or Holy Week, so we had to miss a year.

A NEW VENUE?

In 2013 the College became an Academy and planned a major re-building project to start late in 2015, which would prevent us using any of the site for the following three years. At the same time, the John Fowler Holiday Park was sold to another holiday company, resulting in considerable renovation and changes. We had been hoping we would be back in full swing by 2020 at the latest, but sadly for a whole variety of reasons, the re-built Academy is no longer suitable for us, and the improved Holiday Park has introduced restrictions which make it unsuitable and too expensive for many families. So we have been looking elsewhere for a suitable venue for a week-long CELEBRATE.

REGIONAL WEEKENDS

In 2008, a very late Easter had prevented us holding CELEBRATE at the usual time, as the College students went back on Easter Tuesday, so we had decided to organise a number of non-residential CELEBRATE Regional Weekends in different parts of the country. These covered Saturdays and Sundays and were organised by local teams made up of people

who had attended the main Conference and demonstrated
an interest and commitment to all that CELEBRATE stood for.
The first Regional Weekends were held in St. Albans,
Southampton, the North West, Guildford (now Twickenham),
and Bristol. They proved popular and successful, typically
attracting between 250 and 550 participants each, with the
result that over the following years Weekends were added in
Brighton, Cardiff, Cleethorpes, Taunton (now Plymouth),
Newcastle upon Tyne, East Anglia, Birmingham and Glasgow.
The Weekends keep to the CELEBRATE vision, providing
streams for children of different ages. **Joel's Bar** (the
CELEBRATE group for young adults) also run an annual week
at Worth Abbey, which attracts about 200 aged between
seventeen and thirty. The event is supported by the
Benedictine Community, who invite the young people to join
them for their regular prayer times during the day. The week
helps those who attend to maintain their strong relationships,
provides good teaching, involves worship, fellowship and fun
in a great setting, so not surprisingly it has proved to be very
popular.

RELEASE
One of the challenges arising from the success of the Regional
Weekends is the need to provide teams of qualified leaders for
all the children's streams. So to help meet this need and to
avoid exhausting the small number of qualified leaders we
had, it was decided to train some of our young adults to take
on this responsibility. This led to the birth of RELEASE, a
twelve month part-time programme of leadership training for

about 30 young people. The training consists of special weekends and days, supported by materials provided on-line, practical experience, with individual mentors and account-ability partners. So far more than 100 young leaders have been trained and now work to resource the streams at the Regional Weekends, but beyond that they are equipped to serve the Church more widely. 'Celebrate@home' is another initiative which is being developed with teaching resources for use in small groups and parishes for local families to build relationships, enjoy praise and worship, receive good teaching, and come together with all ages in the family, including times for food and relaxation in what has become the CELEBRATE Tradition.

IMPORTANT CONTRIBUTIONS
One of the features of the CELEBRATE Conferences and Weekends is the amazing selection of books and spiritual reading which Gerard and Toni Pomfret of Good News Books display as a bookshop, bringing to full effect the initial very promising work of the late Vivian Sewell and her helpers. Another feature are the recordings of the talks and workshops made by Archie and Cathy Cameron of Agape Ministries, thereby making all the excellent teaching available to people who were not able to be present. We are most grateful for these really helpful contributions to all the CELEBRATE events. From the very beginning we have also encouraged drama and mime in our main sessions. These creative expressions of our faith have proved to be extremely popular – due in no small measure to the brilliant Christian mimes presented by our

good friend Steve Murray, which are a great source of
inspiration to all who see them. The drama group RISE Theatre
began at CELEBRATE in Ilfracombe when Charley Pinfold and
Hannah Martin presented a couple of sketches with our
encouragement. From these simple beginnings RISE Theatre
is now a professional drama group, presenting the Gospel in
churches and schools all over the country.

BACK-SEAT FOUNDERS
So CELEBRATE continues to flourish and develop, whilst
the Management Team are searching for a venue for a new
week-long Conference, and are constantly reviewing the
original vision and aims to ensure we are in tune with the way
ahead, inspired and guided by the Holy Spirit. As the original
visionaries and founders, Sue and I have maintained a very
active involvement as CELEBRATE has grown and developed
with the commitment of the Management Team, involving key
individuals like Jenny Baker, who leads the Team and works
tirelessly to resource, maintain, guide and challenge every area
of CELEBRATE'S ministry. The team currently consists of
Gemma Wildsmith, Anne Nolan, Andrew Fava, Claire
Fernandes, Pippa Baker, Rachel Mannix, Andrew Grundy, and
Yvonne Watts, with Andy Drozdziak who looks after the
website. David Payne, Peter Moran, Tim Stevens and Sarah
Goldsmith were active members earlier, and there will
certainly be some new members by the time you read this.
Financially the Lord has blessed us with the resources needed,
and we have a number of faithful donors who ensure that the
ministry will continue. Sue and I have recently stepped back

from active involvement, leaving that to the younger team, but as the Founders we remain totally committed and will attend as many Weekends as we can as normal participants or guest speakers. Each Weekend is organised by its own local team who are responsible for all the planning and administration, with the important aim of also breaking even financially, overseen by the Management Team. An unexpected fruit has been the establishment of CELEBRATE Family Conferences in Holland, Austria, and Canada. They are each independent and all that is asked of them is that they follow the documented CELEBRATE Vision.

THE CELEBRATE SAILING MISSION 2019

I could not ignore the most amazing event of 2019, when Russ Fairman, a tireless CELEBRATE helper with his wife Deirdre, undertook the 77 day long **CELEBRATE Sailing Mission,** praying right around the UK coastline. He began in Southampton and sailed his yacht, accompanied by frequently changing skilled or unskilled crew members, and prayed along the south coast to London's Canary Wharf, up the east coast, across the Scottish canal, over to Northern Ireland, down the west coast and back to Southampton. When docking every evening in different harbours, they held prayer meetings, and the Lord did some quite remarkable things during the trip. The yacht had the words 'What if it's true' on its side, which as you can imagine provoked many questions and some great discussions. Truly another amazing and anointed CELEBRATE event! Thank you, Russ!

GOD'S FAITHFULNESS

Over the years of the CELEBRATE Conference, and now of the CELEBRATE Weekends, we have managed to build up financial reserves which offer some security in case any of the events lose money or to fund further expansion. We take up just one Offering at each event, much of which we give away to help in areas of hardship and need, to contribute to individual training initiatives, and in support of the groups and others who come to serve our events. The Lord has blessed CELEBRATE in so many ways including the finances, confirming that we can always rely on Him when we respond to His calling.

THE CELEBRATE VISION

CELEBRATE aims to inspire and equip people of all ages to live an authentic Christian life, and is open to Christians from every part of the body of Christ.

CELEBRATE seeks to:
- Provide an atmosphere of friendship and close fellowship, thereby promoting a real sense of community for formation and mission.

- Celebrate the Liturgy in the best possible way for those present.

- Offer the best available teaching on faith and current issues, based on the Scriptures and the teaching documents of the Catholic Church.

- Include among those invited as speakers men and women from Protestant, Pentecostal, Non-Denominational and New Independent Churches and Fellowships, so that we benefit from their gifts and thereby promote Christian unity.

- Build relationships and increase unity throughout the Catholic Charismatic Renewal.

- Hold to the central truths of the Catholic faith without emphasizing those devotions which are a matter of personal choice.

- Provide spiritually for children, teenagers and young adults in streams or groups according to age or academic year.

- Show our young people in particular that it's exciting, fun and challenging to be a Christian today.

- Encourage on-going friendship among those who attend Celebrate events.

- Give everyone the freedom to be fully Charismatic, while remaining sensitive to those not coming from this faith experience.

- Offer Baptism in the Spirit and Life in the Spirit seminars/workshops.

- Encourage creative activities and use drama, mime, art and music to emphasise the Gospel message.

- Invite everyone to participate in lively praise and worship, and include the exercise of the Gifts of the Spirit.

- Offer personal prayer by trained prayer teams.

- Use money raised in the Celebrate Offerings to sponsor training and development for individuals, communities, groups and special ministries.

- Promote and support an awareness of social, moral, ethical and justice issues, and provide funds from the Offerings for Christian work in disaster areas.

- Support financially and practically Christian organisations sharing a similar vision and working for renewal of the church.

- Offer training and leadership opportunities.

SEVENTEEN

ONE FOR THE BOYS!

I N 1994 I WENT TO NOVA SCOTIA TO SPEAK at a diocesan
weekend Catholic Charismatic conference, and on the
Friday evening as we assembled for the first session I
noticed there were a good number of men present – a much
higher percentage than I was used to seeing at similar events.
Sitting next to the Bishop who had invited me, I referred to this
and asked him if it was normal. He told me that because he
had been concerned about the very small number of men
coming to events like this, he had decided to do something
about it, so had organised a special weekend for men only, to
be led by a team from Renewal Ministries, Ann Arbor. In spite
of the fact that only a small number of men signed up, it had
been a remarkable success so he invited the Ann Arbor team
to come back a year later. This time a large number of men
attended, inspired by the witness of the changes in the men
who had been there the previous year, and had been set on fire
by the Holy Spirit. I could clearly see the fruit of this in front
of me.

THE BIRTH OF HARVESTERS

So I began to think about trying something similar back at
home and called together a small group of leaders to see what
they thought of the idea. Their response was unanimously
positive and after several prayerful planning meetings, our
first Weekend for Men was launched in July 1997 at

Woldingham School in Surrey. We had decided not to invite any outside group to facilitate this, but did it ourselves in new and creative ways. We had been gathering for our planning meetings at a Harvesters pub in West London, so the event rather naturally took on the title 'A Harvesters Weekend for Men', and we were delighted when almost 200 men signed up. The majority were Catholics with a few from other churches, and the event was a great success – far exceeding our expectations and hopes. Our small team consisted of Fr. Mike Gwinnell, David Payne, Roy Hendy, Iain Archibald, Mike Shaughnessy and myself, and we led the weekend with a couple of guest speakers. Those who attended encouraged us to make such weekends regular events, so we put on Harvesters Weekends around the country in places like the University of Lancaster, Stonyhurst College, church premises near Glasgow, and at Woldingham School. In recent years we have focused on one main weekend at the High Leigh Christian Centre in North London, and the numbers have settled at between 70 and 150 men, with larger numbers when we have special speakers like Fr. Raniero Cantalamessa, the Papal Preacher from Rome. One of the most popular parts of the weekends are the small sharing groups, which give the men an opportunity to open up about their own challenges, struggles and blessings in total confidence. Personally I have been disappointed that we have not attracted larger numbers, but on the positive side some local gatherings have been birthed and there are groups of men meeting monthly in their local churches. In my area a dozen or so men from two parishes meet monthly for an evening of worship, fellowship and teaching, with a light meal and a glass of wine. Our current Parish Priest nearly always takes part.

GOOD FRUIT

The annual weekend at High Leigh Centre is always a great experience, attracting a mixture of old and new participants. Those who have been coming are predominantly men in their fifties and above, but we are now attracting a number of younger men, a very positive feature being the group of fathers and sons who attend. One of the most amazing fruits has been in Poland, as some years ago a small group of men had heard about what we were doing and expressed interest, so we invited them to come over and join us as our guests. They so much enjoyed the weekend that they started St. Joseph's Men in Poland, and today they have thousands of men meeting on a regular basis. I have been over to speak to them several times in different parts of the country, and they recently organised a highly successful week-long retreat in Rome. St. Joseph's Men has a real anointing and is a highly encouraging success story of some leaders responding to God's calling.

THE WAY AHEAD

Back at home as I write this, we have entered into a time of change and development, and are looking at ways of attracting more young men to embrace the Harvester's vision. It seems clear that a one-day event will appeal to some of our very busy younger men, so this is likely to feature in our future planning. I have stepped down from my position as Chairman and

Gerard Pomfret has succeeded me, whilst at the same time we have brought some younger men onto the planning committee. None of the original founding group (except the writer) are today involved in the leadership. We are also looking at venues which will be easier for men in the Midlands and North, and which might be less expensive. What will always remain at the heart of what we do is the vision of bringing men of all ages and states of life into a closer and more dynamic relationship with Jesus in the power of the Holy Spirit. From simple beginnings, the Spirit has already brought about some wonderful changes in people's lives and we are so grateful for this. In England both Cor et Lumen Christi Community and Sion Community are regularly organising events for men in different parts of the country, and there are also St. Joseph's Men's groups which took their inspiration from Polish groups, whose leaders in turn had been inspired to start them up in Poland by coming to Harvesters as our guests. We're all in this together and are clearly meeting an important need which Harvesters brought to light in the UK thanks to the vision of my friend, the Bishop in Nova Scotia, in the early 1990s.

MISSIONS TO AFRICA
One of the very positive initiatives to have emerged from Harvesters, is that for several years a group of our men have gone to parts of **Africa** at the invitation of local bishops and clergy, to address groups of parish men and sometimes wider groups of parishioners. These trips are funded from the offerings taken up at our Harvesters UK events, and usually

take place with three men in the autumn or early in the New Year. They are extremely popular with those who go as part of the team, and with the African men who receive their ministry. There are some wonderful accounts of people's faith coming alive, of healings, and of the gifts of the Spirit experienced in action.

HARVESTERS AND THE **CELEBRATE** SAILING MISSION **2019**
Russ Fairman, who recently sailed his yacht on the CELEBRATE Sailing Mission for 77 days right around the UK coast in prayer for the country and for CELEBRATE, is also a key member of the Harvesters Team, so they prayed for Harvesters too. I have mentioned it here because Russ was a main speaker at our last Harvesters Weekend and talked about the amazing things the Lord did on this CELEBRATE Sailing Mission.

Where the Spirit will lead us in the future remains to be seen, but it is clear that for a good number of men, the Harvester's Weekends have provided a much-needed opportunity for fellowship, teaching and ministry in a charismatic environment. Definitely 'one for the boys!'

EIGHTEEN

CALLED TO SERVE

W E ALL NEED TO KNOW WHAT GOD IS CALLING US TO DO for Him – then we can take our proper place in His Church. He may call us from one thing into something else, and it is a call which will shape our lives. We have been called into His Kingdom *(1 Peter 2:9)* to live as disciples of Jesus, but a time will come when He will reveal His particular will and purpose for each of us individually. I have learned that I need to hold on to whatever vision God gives me. As the Word reminds us: *'Write down the revelation and make it plain. For the revelation awaits an appointed time. Though it linger, wait for it' (Habbakuk 2:2-3).* God calls some of His followers to be leaders, others into full-time Christian work and this should be seen as a privilege, as something He has clearly initiated, and for which He will equip us with the gifts and skills needed. To be an effective Christian leader requires that I am called by God, and He often calls unlikely people into positions of influence and authority. This means I have to remain totally dependent on Him and not on my own ideas and abilities. There is no substitute for God's will. In the early 1980s I recognised that God was calling me into Christian leadership and that He was going to prepare me and equip me for my calling. I've described how some of this occurred in earlier chapters, and I still think back in wonder to the time I had an office in Vatican premises and regular meetings with Pope St. John Paul II, often after being at his private early morning Mass.

A FOOT-WASHING MINISTRY

Christian leadership is a big subject. All Christian leaders are called to be servants – it's a foot-washing ministry and this makes it very different from the world's ideas of leadership. But there are many different types of Christian leaders, so I want to consider from my own experience what is distinctive about leaders in Charismatic Renewal. This is important, because good leadership will ensure that the CCR plays an increasingly important part in the life of the Church, whereas bad leadership will restrict us to the fringes. Since the arrival of CHARIS we have a great opportunity to give good leadership and we must take it. We need to be sure our leaders are faithful to their calling and open to the guidance of the Spirit, not just to pastor the Renewal but to bring the charisms into the life of the whole Church. This is Pope Francis' second objective in the CHARIS Statutes.

THE POWER OF THE SPIRIT

One thing is immediately clear – to lead in the Charismatic Renewal we need to have personally had a powerful experience of the presence and the power of the Holy Spirit, the gateway to a new life of faith and confidence. How it happens is not important – but it must happen. Baptism in the Spirit provides the power to witness and to serve, a new ability in prayer, a willingness to suffer rejection for Christ, a clearer understanding and a love for the Scriptures, and an entrance into spiritual gifts. None of these things came through my own ability – all of them depended on the grace of God through the presence of His Spirit. But the most wonderful result is a deeper love for the Lord and for one another. To be a leader in the Charismatic Renewal I had to have a personal experience of the transforming power of the Spirit of God.

THE CHARISMATIC GIFTS

There are of course many gifts of God, but one of the distinguishing marks of the Charismatic Renewal is an experience and an acceptance of the charismatic gifts listed in *1 Corinthians 12* and emphasised in *Lumen Gentium 12*, the Vatican II document on the nature and mystery of the Church. Why is this important? Because in much of the Church today there is ignorance, suspicion and neglect of these supernatural manifestations of the power of God, just as there was in some places during the time of St. Paul. We need to show that the charisms are to be used in love to serve others and to build up the Church, and that they have always been an officially accepted part of the teaching of the Church. Charisms are not to be sought for themselves – the Lord gives them to us for the transformation, healing and blessing of others. So we charismatic leaders must be clearly taught about these gifts and how to use them. By her very nature the Church is both hierarchical and charismatic – both are essential for her life and ministry. If the Church was only hierarchical it would be authoritarian, boring, and slowly dying. If it was only charismatic it would be wonderfully exciting, but totally chaotic and confusing. Both are essential for a healthy Church. When the power of the Spirit is released within us He reveals our Father and Jesus in a new way, brings us power and authority, and equips us to serve in an effective way. It is important that we realise it is not just a matter of living the old life in a more exciting way – it introduces a completely new principle of conduct. From now on all our actions will proceed from the life of the Spirit within us, not just from the principles of good behavior and performance.

WORLDLY LEADERSHIP

In my own experience, I went from Durham University in 1965 to work in the paper industry, initially in Manchester and then in London. I stayed with the same company until my retirement in 2000, but only worked part-time from 1989 onwards. I had a very successful career in the UK paper industry and I have written more about this in chapter 4. I am mentioning it again because it gave me invaluable experience and training in ethical worldly leadership and was clearly part of God's plan for my life, helping me enormously when He called me into leadership in the Charismatic Renewal, my parish and diocese from 1982 onwards. Much of what I had learned in industry about human relationships was helpful when I brought it under the guidance and power of the Holy Spirit.

AN OPEN DOOR

One of the fascinating challenges from the early 1980s onwards, was also how to apply the lessons I was learning in the Charismatic Renewal to my work as a leader in industry. I wanted to help and to bless the people working for me and with me, but not to do so with the authority that came with my position as their Managing Director, which might cause them to accept something they would normally have declined. It seemed to me that the best way to approach this would be to make it clear that I was always available and happy to offer help and advice with any problems they might be facing – at work or in their private lives. As I put this into practice, symbolised by the open door into my office, several of my staff availed themselves of the opportunity to come and talk to me about difficult and painful incidents in their lives, ranging from the accidental death of a much-loved pet to someone in a committed relationship leaving to live with someone else. Often all I could do was to listen with concern and sympathy, but there were occasions when it was possible to offer a short prayer and some practical help. In general I was very aware that I had become much more concerned for the well-being and happiness of all my staff and work colleagues, and was always willing to put myself out if there was some way in which I could help. Of course everyone knew that my Christian faith lay behind all that I was and did, and whilst this caused some amusement – *'Watch out, here comes the Vicar!'* – the main result was that they took the opportunity to benefit from it when they faced difficulties. We occasionally travelled around Sweden by bus, visiting our paper mills as a group. I discovered that I really needed to sit on the back seat of the bus, as colleagues often came to chat privately about issues they were facing. Perhaps the fact that now, twenty years after I retired, about 12 of my old office staff still arrange for us all to have lunch together annually says something very encouraging about our relationships.

Challenges and Refreshment

Even when we are sure we are doing God's will, every leader will face times of testing and difficulty. We must not be surprised when this happens – the Lord will use every occasion for our formation *(Romans 8:28)*. But there are also special times when the Lord chooses to refresh us sovereignly and gloriously by soaking us in the love and power of the Spirit. This can happen at any time and in any place, but it often happens among people who have learned to lay down their defences and to pray with all their hearts *'Come, Holy Spirit!'* The Lord provides such times of refreshment because He knows how much we need them *(Isaiah 43:20-21)* and need to provide them for others. We must learn to enjoy them and to encourage others to drink again and again from the refreshing water of the Spirit.

Life-Changing People of God

As I look back over my life, I see how important were so many of the things that happened, from my times with the nuns at Talacre Abbey when I was a toddler, my Jesuit education, meeting Sue at Durham University, having wonderful children, knowing Christians from other churches and fellowships, my meetings with people like Mother Teresa, Popes John Paul II and Francis, and events like the Azusa Street Centennial Celebrations. But equally important have been the times when I have listened to life-changing teaching and had one-to-one discussions with God's anointed and specially chosen men and women. There are many who have inspired and guided me over the years, but foremost among them are Rev. Jim Graham, our local Baptist minister and the best Bible teacher I have ever heard; Fr. Ian Petit OSB, a fine teacher and a pioneer in the Catholic Charismatic Renewal; Fr. Bob de Grandis, for his approach to the gifts of the Spirit; Pastor John Wimber, another great exponent of the charismatic gifts and the founder of the Vineyard churches; Fr. Raniero Cantalamessa, the preacher to three consecutive Papal Households; Fr. Peter Hocken, a visionary in the work for Christian unity and relations with the Messianic Jews; Reverend Nicky Gumbel, faithful promoter of the ALPHA Course, including ALPHA for Catholics; and Canon Michael Harper, a tireless worker for the development of Charismatic Renewal and Unity throughout the whole body of Christ. Ian, Raniero, and Peter stayed with us at home; John and Carol Wimber invited us to stay with them at their home in California but sadly John became ill so we could not go. Carol later invited me to speak at the London Thanksgiving Service for John's life. Jim Graham gave me my first invitation to speak in a Protestant church, and Michael Harper involved me in the leadership of most of the big ecumenical events he initiated from 1985 onwards. In all our lives there are particular people God has placed there to inspire, teach, help and guide us, and I am so grateful for each one of those mentioned here. I have also been greatly blessed by reading the daily reflections of two great Protestant preachers – Billy Graham and Smith Wigglesworth, both of whom are wonderful gifts to the body of Christ. At the age of 48 Smith Wigglesworth was baptised in the Holy Spirit and his ministry was transformed – a great encouragement that he was more than halfway through his life when this happened, clearly at God's appointed time.

LEVELS OF LEADERSHIP

When it comes to my own leadership in the Church, this has been at local, national and international level, and each brings its own particular challenges and opportunities. Leading a local prayer group involves close and intimate relationships with people I see on a regular basis – they know me and I know them. The challenge I often faced was to take a step back to try to see things with the Lord's eyes, and to ask Him for a prophetic word or insight, which He often granted. At national level the challenges are different, but I am still usually dealing with individuals who carry responsibility for specific projects or groups. Then at international level the challenges become more complicated – language, culture, politics, ambition – how do I cope with all these things when I am an outsider?

HIS CHOSEN CHANNEL

At all levels the answer to the challenges will be the same – I must put myself into the hands of the Lord and try to see the situation as He sees it. I have to know that I am His chosen channel through whom the Holy Spirit will minister to those I have been called to lead. God's will and purpose are all that matter in every situation – He has chosen me, put me in this particular situation, and I can have total confidence that He will guide me in what He wants me to say and do. The most common prayer of most leaders is simply *'Help me, Lord!'* When I was President of the International Catholic Charismatic Renewal Council, travelling all over the world, I often found myself in situations where several people were looking to me to support their particular positions. But the Lord was faithful, and I could always rely on His guidance, even when I knew this was contrary to the popular position. I learned to trust Him completely, no matter how unexpected His position seemed to be. Do I really think I know better than God? Of course not. There will be times when we need to work things out for ourselves, but these are only when God knows we will come to the right conclusion, **His** conclusion, and do things in His way and in His power. Even as I write this, I am conscious that the Lord always has His will and His purposes, but for some reason He has chosen and anointed me as one of His particular instruments and channels to make things happen as He has already decided.

CALLED TO SERVE

In this chapter I have avoided discussing any particular leadership situations in which I have been involved, and this is because I do not want anyone to focus on a particular event. But I do serve as a Trustee for a number of Catholic bodies and groups. These include the Metanoia Project with Ruth and Joe White, which has established a very important youth ministry in parishes in the Preston area; the Pilgrims Community, which was started in Nottingham by Fr. Jonathan Cotton, offering community life and experience in evangelisation and mission to young people; and the Catholic Bible School, established by Joan le Morvan and developed by Geoff and Gina Poulter followed by David and Sarah Beresford, and now producing a range of Bible reading resources for individuals and parishes or groups, which are extremely important in the Church today. Each of these three bodies were birthed through the Charismatic Renewal and have brought their experience of this into practical expression in the life of the Church, and this is how it should be.

Let me conclude this chapter by saying that in my experience God often calls us to things to which we have a natural leaning. Many people strive and strain to be something God never called them to be. They confuse natural gifting with ministry calling. Natural gifting is available to all of us and helps us to do what God is asking in our everyday lives, whereas a ministry calling comes to me personally from the Lord and sets me apart for a particular service, usually involving leadership. God knew me before I was born *(Psalm 139:13-16)* and has always had His hand upon my life. He has prepared me for where I am today – I just have to learn to recognise His voice and to respond to His promptings; not always the easiest thing to do.

NINETEEN
LOVE ONE ANOTHER

Y PERSONAL INVOLVEMENT IN THE WHOLE AREA of Christian unity has been considerable, as Sue is a committed Anglican and I am Catholic. When we both came to a living faith in 1976, we did so primarily through the ministry of Anglicans and Baptists, and so naturally we asked the Lord where He wanted us to be. Quite independently we both heard Him say *'Bloom where you were planted'*, so that is what we are trying to do, me as a Catholic and Sue as an Anglican. Of course we both know that part of the work to which the Lord has called us is to build unity throughout the whole body of Christ. But we also believe it is important that we follow the current rules laid down by the Catholic Church when it comes to receiving Communion. For example, Sue comes to Mass with me on Sundays and comes forward for a prayer of blessing when I receive Communion, and on Wednesday mornings I go with her to our local Anglican church where she receives Communion and I have a prayer of blessing. I must say, the Anglican clergy are mostly very good at praying for someone on these occasions, whereas some of the Catholic priests could do with a bit of help and guidance! The fact that we do not receive Communion together in each other's churches is always very painful, and reminds us that there is still a lot of work to do before we have complete unity.

In several chapters I have written about very specific instances of the work for Christian unity in which I have been involved, usually with Sue. In chapter 12, I explained some of the things that came about through my involvement in ICCOWE; in chapter 13 I looked at the important bi-annual gatherings in Rome with leaders from the New Charismatic Churches; chapter 14 introduced my co-chairmanship of the UK Charismatic and Pentecostal Leaders Conference; and chapter 15 was about the amazing Pentecostal Azusa Street Centennial. So now in this chapter I want to look briefly at the current position of the Catholic Church on ecumenism and to apply that personally.

A TOTAL TRANSFORMATION

The Catholic approach to ecumenism has changed out of all recognition during my lifetime, and as I write this in the papacy of Francis, the pace of change is accelerating all the time. In the first half of the twentieth century the Catholic Church actively discouraged ecumenism, in spite of the efforts of some pioneers like Abbe Paul Couturier, Dom Lambert Beaudouin, and Blessed Maria Gabriella Sagheddu who is the Patron of the Ecumenical Movement. During the time of Pope Pius XI it was clearly stated in 1928 in a papal document entitled 'Mortalium Animos' that it was fundamentally wrong to pray with other Christians, and the embryonic ecumenical movement was condemned and stifled. When I started school in 1947 at a local Anglican Primary, I had to leave the morning assembly every day when it came to the time for prayers to be said. But in 1948 things began to change, and a statement came from the Vatican to say that 'the growing desire for unity is under the Holy Spirit', and prayer together was to be encouraged. So our parish priest, Fr. Mooney, came to our house for tea to tell me that I could now remain in the morning school assembly for the prayers, and I fully believed that the Pope had sent him round to tell me this! So we were starting to move forward in the whole area of relationships with our 'separated brethren'.

THE RESTORATION OF UNITY

But it was when the Second Vatican Council started to discuss ecumenism that a completely new approach was born in 1964 – 'Unitatis Redintegratio, the Restoration of Unity'. The very first sentence of this document contains a definitive statement: '*The restoration of unity among all Christians is one of the principal concerns of the Second Vatican Council*', and in the first paragraph we are reminded that '*Division openly contradicts the will of Christ, scandalises the world, and damages the holy cause of preaching the Gospel to every creature.*' Having laid a framework in the document for a new commitment to working for unity, the Council then encouraged all Catholics to become actively involved: '*The Sacred Council exhorts all the Catholic faithful to recognize the signs of the times and to take an active and intelligent part in the work of ecumenism*'. '*It is desirable that Catholics should join in prayer with their separated brethren. Such prayers in common are certainly an effective means of obtaining the grace of unity*'. Pope St. John XXIII had always wanted this reality to be promoted by the Council, and must have been delighted.

LIVING IN HARMONY

In *Matthew 18:19* Jesus Himself tells His disciples: *'Again, I tell you that if two of you on earth agree about anything you ask for, it will be done for you by My Father in Heaven.'* That is quite a statement Jesus makes and however I may look at it or seek to qualify it, I can't get away from the message that unity releases power. That's one reason why I find the translation of *Psalm 133* in The New Living Bible really encouraging:

How wonderful and pleasant it is, when brothers live together in harmony! For harmony is as precious as the anointing oil that was poured over Aaron's head, that ran down his beard and onto the border of his robe. Harmony is as refreshing as the dew from Mount Hermon that falls in the mountains of Zion, and there the Lord has pronounced His blessing, even life everlasting.

We all need to live in harmony – with ourselves, with God, with our families and friends, within our Christian communities, with those of other Faiths and of different ethnic backgrounds and cultures. While full Christian unity is always our goal, harmony is something we can achieve more easily. Harmony means that we can work together with a common purpose, but without having to agree on everything. God describes this as wonderful, pleasant, precious and refreshing, and that's where He has pronounced His blessing. It's very releasing to know that I can be in harmony with others without full unity. It allows me to make room in my life for the other person, and harmony will lead us closer to unity.

EMPOWERED BY UNITY

Sue and I went to speak in Northern Ireland several times during the violent period before the Peace Process began, and have spoken on Christian unity in a number of countries around the world. It seems that having opened a door for this, the Holy Spirit uses one speaking engagement to open another door, then another. For example, as a direct result of building close personal friendships with a Swedish Pastor and his wife, a number of study tours of Rome developed where we took groups of up to forty of their European Evangelical leaders to visit the historic churches and Christian sites, to meet officials in the Council for Promoting Christian Unity, to a General Audience with Pope Benedict, and to have theological discussions with men like Fr. Raniero Cantalamessa. Sue and I were then invited to speak in the Pastor's church in Sweden, and in all these meetings we prayed, shared, worshipped the Lord together and became friends. There were amazing releases of the power of the Spirit in breaking down walls of mistrust, misunderstandings and straightforward hostility which had existed for years. We experienced the power of the Spirit in our unity as brothers and sisters in Christ. The Lord has since led our friends Pastor Ulf Ekman and his wife Birgitta to become active members of the Catholic Church.

As a result of speaking in Ulf's Swedish Evangelical church, we were seen on the internet in Norway, and invited by a Pentecostal Pastor to visit three cities, where he with the local Catholic priests and Lutheran ministers brought their congregations together for the first time. Barriers were broken, relationships were established, and they have continued to hold regular meetings together. Because we went to Norway, a pastor in America read about the meetings and saw them on a DVD, so we received an invitation to speak at the preparations of an organisation called 'The Church in the City' in San Antonio, Texas. A number of San Antonio churches – Catholic, Protestant, Pentecostal and Independent – were getting together to build unity in preparation for a city-wide ecumenical mission. This had the full support of the local Catholic bishop, and a cross-section of churches were already beginning to work together. A group of leaders were praying together weekly and had been Prayer-Walking the streets together, resulting in a remarkable fall in both crime and vandalism, to the delight of the police and the city authorities. There is such Holy Spirit power in unity!

Whilst in San Antonio we were invited to speak in a Pentecostal church on a Sunday morning, and when we arrived there we discovered they had never had a Catholic speaker, and many of the church members were Spanish speaking ex-Catholics. We shared our testimonies and then talked about the Holy Spirit working in our lives, and at the end were overwhelmed by the numbers coming forward for prayer and to ask forgiveness for their negative views of Catholics.

One of the Lord's surprises was that a local councilor had come that morning to invite the congregation to a special event put on by the Council. He turned out to be a Catholic too, but had never heard of baptism in the Holy Spirit before and wanted to hear more about it!

FAMILY DISAGREEMENTS

But in any natural family there are often disagreements between parents and children, brothers and sisters, fathers and sons, mothers and daughters – however the family relationship is still there, it is not destroyed by our disagreements. So it should be between brothers and sisters in Christ – Anglicans, Baptists, Catholics, Pentecostals, Independent Christians. By our shared baptism and our acknowledgement of Jesus Christ as our Lord and Saviour, we **are** brothers and sisters in Christ and the Catholic Church recognises this fact as stated in the Catechism section 818. Furthermore *'Christian unity is the business of all Christians regardless of how young or old they are'* *(YouCat 131)*. Pope St. John Paul II felt called by the Lord to write his amazing encyclical *'Ut Unum Sint'* on Christian unity, and Pope Benedict XVI said at the beginning of his papacy that unity was a top priority. For Pope Francis too, ecumenism has the highest importance and he continually emphasises that we must work together now – we cannot wait until we are one. After expressing his total appreciation for the work of theologians in this area, he once went on jokingly to say that we should not wait for them to come to an agreement, but should already be doing as much as possible together because if we waited for the theologians Christ could well have returned before they solved all the problems!

AN ECUMENICAL GRACE

Among Pope Francis' stated expectations for the Catholic Charismatic Renewal we find: *'Give witness of spiritual ecumenism with all those brothers and sisters of other churches and Christian communities who believe in Jesus as Lord and Saviour. The Charismatic Renewal is by its very nature ecumenical'.* He clearly sees Renewal in the Spirit as an ecumenical grace, a view which echoes Pope St. John Paul II:

> *'...by your experience of the many gifts of the Holy Spirit which are also shared with our separated brothers and sisters, yours is the special joy of growing in a desire for the unity to which the Spirit guides us and in a commitment to the serious work of ecumenism'.*

It's also interesting to note that Pope Francis believes that the Reformation was really over in 1999, when the Catholic Church and the Lutheran Church Federation issued a joint declaration on justification *'by God's grace through faith in Christ'.*

RECEPTIVE ECUMENISM

Before he was elected Pope, Sue and I had been down to Buenos Aires to meet Cardinal Bergoglio, as I mentioned in an earlier chapter. Our reason was that in Latin America, it was Buenos Aires where the relationships between Catholic and Pentecostal leaders could be described as good, and this was because Bergoglio had established personal friendships with a number of their leaders and pastors. He strongly believes that we should be doing together as much as we can, and since becoming Pope he has continued to meet informally with Protestant, Pentecostal and Independent leaders on a regular basis, often speaking of **'receptive ecumenism'**, firm in his conviction that we all have gifts to share.

ANNIVERSARY CELEBRATIONS

At the 50th anniversary celebrations of the Catholic Charismatic Renewal in 2017 in Rome, Pope Francis was insistent that leaders from all the other charismatic churches would be there 'as of right', not just because we invited them. So on the platform in the Circus Maximus on the eve of Pentecost they were seated in the rows behind him. Sue and I were asked to be up there too, because we were a good example of an ecumenical marriage, and one of those he asked to speak was his Italian Pentecostal friend, Giovanni Traettino.

FROM CONFLICT TO COMMITMENT

As Christians we are hopefully following a process in our relationships with other churches which could be described as the 'C' Scale. According to this scale, we move steadily from:

- Conflict to Competition
- Competition to Co-existence
- Co-existence to Co-operation
- Co-operation to Commitment
- Commitment to Communion – one day, please God!

It can be helpful to identify where our own local church is on this scale.

SOME PRINCIPLES

Here are ten simple principles which have helped me in my ecumenical work:-

1. Accept one another as brothers and sisters in Christ.

2. Be faithful to who you are, and sure about what your Church teaches.

3. Remember that there are differences, but more unites than separates us.

4. Repent for our differences – forgive and ask forgiveness together.

5. Listen – it shows respect; we have to learn what others believe and why.

6. Build and protect close personal relationships.

7. Accept that there is a healthy tension between Love and Truth, but remember that Love is the authentic sign of true Christianity.

8. Recognise that there is a price to be paid in the work for unity.

9. Do as much together as we can in good conscience.

10. Never forget – Jesus and the Father want unity, and it's a work of the Spirit.

The work for unity among all Christians presents us with a major challenge, but it can be achieved. We know this because of the prayer of Jesus:

> **'A new command I give you: Love one another. As I have loved you, so you must love one another. By this all men will know that you are my disciples, if you love one another' (John 13:34-35).**

Jesus only ever asks us to do something which He knows we are capable of doing. But only in **His** strength and not by our own will-power because we can be absolutely certain that Christian unity is God's will for **all** His children.

TWENTY

ALL THINGS IN CHRIST

THE PACE OF LIFE TODAY IS VERY FAST, and there seems so much to do all the time. Being married and bringing up a family is wonderful, exciting, challenging and demanding. A working life, whether in the world of commerce and business, in the professions, in charity work and areas of service, or in some special ministry, is going to be demanding and time-consuming. If we add in voluntary work, our routine service in the Church, and the personal relationships involved in each of these areas which are so critical for success, it's amazing that we can survive and keep going. And of course the risks are that one or another important area will suffer some neglect.

A VERY FULL LIFE

When I began seriously working in the Charismatic Renewal from 1978 onwards, I already had a full-time job working for my Swedish forestry and paper company, and because I have never been one to sit back and take things easy, I was also involved in a lot of linked activities as I have described earlier, all requiring meetings and my personal participation. My secular work alone meant that I travelled around the UK, with regular visits to the parent company in Sweden and to my colleagues in various European countries. To this very full programme, I added meetings and events as part of my Church work and ministry, all of which led to another of the Lord's miraculous interventions!

A CHANGE IN MY WORK

In the late 1980s my Church commitments were demanding more and more of my time, and I began thinking about resigning from my job and doing only part-time paid work. Whilst I was thinking about this I attended a conference in Rome in May, where one morning I found myself queuing for coffee next to my friend Fr. Bob Faricy, an American priest lecturing in Rome. He asked me how things were going and I simply replied that I was finding doing all that I had to do very challenging. *'I'll pray for you'* he said cheerfully, and went off with his coffee. Two days later he came to me: *'The Lord has a word for you. You must resign from your job at the end of August and by Christmas His purposes for you will be clear'*.

In August we were on holiday as a family in Tenby, Wales, and every morning I took a long walk on the beach and prayed about the future. As a result I handed in my resignation at the end of the month. My boss in Sweden telephoned me to say that he absolutely did not want me to leave, but as my contracted notice period was twelve months we would discuss it later. He came to see me on December 18th and offered to maintain my employment and position on a part-time basis – could I accept this? He needed my answer by Christmas as he was going away on holiday. I telephoned him on December 22nd and said yes, and that I was assuming he would pay me half my current salary. *'I never said that'* he replied, and so I thought he was going to offer me less. *'I'll continue to pay you a full salary'* he said. Amazingly all the subsidiary companies for which I was responsible performed even better when I was only working part-time - we just need to trust the Lord and to do what He asks.

THE FAMILY

Life remained very full, with a lot of travel increased by my worldwide responsibilities as President of ICCRS during the 1990s. I enjoyed the travel, the conferences and meetings, so I was never slow to respond positively to the many important invitations I received, and of course I also had the office at the Vatican where I needed to spend time. So what about the family – Sue and our four wonderful children, one daughter and three sons? We had our first two children, Lucy and Adam, quite soon after we were married, and they were born just a year apart. Our second two, Luke and Tom, came about ten years later after our faith had come alive, so we always look upon them as a particular sign of God's blessing. They are now all living happy and successful lives, and we are the proud grandparents of six grandchildren and two step-grandchildren.

SOME REGRETS

We did our best to maintain a reasonable family life, to be present at all the important occasions for our children, to have good holidays – Llangranog for several years, Tenby, Denmark, Sweden, Paris, the South of France, Anglesey and North Wales – and to do things together. But I fully acknowledge that there were times when I should have been present, but was not. Once missed, these occasions are lost forever – they cannot be brought back. Do I regret this? Yes, I do, and if I had my time over again I would do my best to make some changes. I am fortunate that my children have faithfully supported me in all that I have done, and we remain in good, loving relationships with them and their other halves, but I know there are things I should have done which I failed to do. Maintaining a good balance in our lives is always important, but is often hard to achieve. I am not a person who finds big crowds relaxing, so free weekends were often times when I wanted to do very little. The Lord always wants to help us have a good balance in our lives, and I am grateful for the times I received His guidance. Once the children grew up, Sue was able to accompany me on more of my trips and this has been and remains a great joy. All four of our children are living good and upright lives, without having come to a personal, active life of faith in Jesus Christ. But we know God is close to all our family, and we trust them into His loving care.

DIVINE HEALING

An amazing example of His care was Luke's healing from deafness. Luke suffered from high frequency deafness which adversely affected his speech, and the medical profession could only offer lip-reading as a help. Of course we prayed for his healing, but there was no change. When he was about four years old, Pentecostal Pastor John Barr came to stay locally at the home of a friend, and before leaving he gave a talk on healing to which Sue was invited. Inspired by his words, she received a gift of faith that this was the time for Luke to be healed, collected him from playschool, and asked John to pray for him. She also asked him to pray about Luke's hat, because he always wore a cap – he wore it all day, in bed, in the bath, when he went swimming – he refused to take it off. John prayed in tongues and then cast out the spirit of deafness from Luke. He went on to ask the Lord to take away the fear Luke had of something falling on his head. On the way home Luke told Sue that when the man had prayed for him his ears began to hurt. Entering the house, Luke took off the cap and never ever wore it again. That night in the dark, Sue spoke words to Luke that he had never been able to hear – he not only heard them but was able to repeat them perfectly. When the doctor checked him, he had absolutely perfect hearing. He had been delivered of an evil spirit and totally healed, and because he no longer wore his cap, lots of people wanted to know why not – a wonderful opportunity to tell them what the Lord had done!

DOING GOD'S WILL

I knew that after I experienced baptism in the Spirit and my faith had come alive in a new way, the Lord could change anything and everything. But I also knew that He never takes away our free will and I could always say 'no' or simply ignore whatever I thought He was saying to me. I may claim to be open to the work of the Spirit in and through me, but I have to make sure that I am open to whatever He does – not just to what I want Him to do. Am I willing to let go of what I want if it's not God's will for me? My relationship with God lies at the heart of everything I am and do; it is even more important than my human relationships, and I must never forget this. When I'm doing His will He will take care of me and those who are dependent on me.

KEY PERSONAL RELATIONSHIPS
In everything I have been writing about, everything I have experienced over the last forty or so years, there are personal relationships with all sorts of very different people. Every single one of us is involved in different sorts of relationships in each area of our lives – we cannot avoid this. Whether it's within the family, which are of course our most important relationships, with our friends, at church, in our work, in our hobbies and recreational pursuits – we all have to interact with lots of very different people. With some of them it will be easy – there will be natural levels of contact through personality, intellectual capacity, physical ability, and outlook on life. With others it will be more difficult – we will see things differently and lack any natural feelings of unity or shared experience. This is all absolutely to be expected – God created each of us as a unique human being, with our own particular nature, capacity, interests and way of seeing things.

WHAT DRAWS US TOGETHER?
When we look at the Apostles and disciples of Jesus, they were a really mixed bunch – Peter and later Paul, John and Matthew, James – but their shared commitment to Jesus joined them together in unity. So when we look at our relationships today, what is it that draws us together? If we work together in the same profession or commercial organisation, we will have shared values and common aims. If we relax together and share the same sport, or support the same team or club, we will have shared hopes and dreams. If we are part of the same natural family, we will share in physical relationships, have a

common history, and probably shared hopes for what lies ahead. So what does all this mean when it comes to building good personal relationships with all those who are part of our lives in one way or another? It simply means that as Christians we need to look for the best in everyone we meet, to see them with the eyes of Christ, to forgive and overlook their weaknesses and short-comings, and to seek to build strong personal relationships in love. In some cases there will be definite limits to what the other will accept, but our challenge is to go to those limits. In other cases it will be possible to build much closer and stronger personal relationships, so we must do this. When it comes to our fellow Christians, the sky really is the limit.

AN IMMEDIATE BOND

Over the years I have met other Christians with whom there has immediately been a sense of unity and common purpose. To move forward with them in a loving and developing relationship has been easy because of the tangible sense of the presence of the Holy Spirit in both our lives. In other cases it has been much harder and a slow process to grow in a personal and loving relationship. If someone has been hurt and suffered rejection after investing time and effort in building a relationship, they will be very cautious before risking themselves again. This is perfectly understandable – we would almost certainly feel the same. But the fact remains that nearly everything depends on the strength and quality of our personal relationships. In families this is very much the case just as anywhere else. There is a legitimate expectation in a family that whatever may happen we will always be accepted and loved. Sue and I always emphasised to our children that whatever happened they would be welcome to come home. We did our best to give them roots and wings – yes, they should fly the nest and make their own ways in life, but whatever might happen they must always feel the freedom to return to their roots – to come home in the certainty that they would be loved and accepted no matter what might have happened. This is exactly what we can expect from our loving Father and from our Lord and Saviour, Jesus Christ. Yes, we may have messed up, we may be totally in the wrong or may have been totally wronged, but our Heavenly Father is always waiting for us with open arms. This is the model for all our relationships too – whether spiritual or natural. We too must be forgiving and accepting towards all those with whom we are in relationship, and paramount among them are the members of our natural family.

AT THE HEART OF IT ALL

If we now look again at our natural relationships, at work, in business or our professional lives as well as in our recreation and hobbies, we need to be working to establish levels of trust, acceptance and friendship that will mean others will feel totally confident in turning to us when things go wrong. Even more should it be true in our church and spiritual relationships, where people must feel absolutely confident in trusting us with every area of their lives. Unless this total trust is present, there is something missing from our relationships. We must be sure to put this right – good relationships are at the heart of everything.

TWENTY ONE

THERE'S ALWAYS MORE!

A
T ITS MOST SIMPLE, WALKING IN THE SPIRIT means walking with God, in complete unity with Him and His purposes, directed and empowered by His Holy Spirit. It means putting into practice day after day the new life that Jesus has made available to me. *'Since we live by the Spirit, let us keep in step with the Spirit' (Galatians 5:25).* Jesus Himself explained it to Nicodemus like this:

> *'I tell you the truth, no-one can enter the Kingdom of God unless he is born of water and the Spirit. Flesh gives birth to flesh, but the Spirit gives birth to spirit. You should not be surprised at my saying 'you must be born again'. The wind blows wherever it pleases. You hear its sound, but you cannot tell where it comes from or where it is going. So it is with everyone born of the Spirit' (John 3:5-8).*

BORN AGAIN

I am born again when I enter this new life through baptism and the coming of the Holy Spirit, but living it out is not automatic. Even though I know all about it and want to walk in the Spirit and enjoy this new life, the old life is still open to me and I must be aware of this. What is the old life? It's a life lived largely by rules. I see Jesus Christ as a man who lived two thousand years ago and I believe that He is God, sent to help me by His Father, and I try to follow His teaching and to do as He did. I take on His ideals and try to live by them. So I see Christianity as a way of life governed by a set of rules, and I try by using my willpower to do whatever is right and to live as I believe Jesus would want me to live. This approach is very similar to that of the Jewish people at the time of Christ: they tried to live by the Law but failed. Even those who wanted to live by the Law could not do so, and those whose task it was to teach the Law also failed to put it into practice in their own lives or to help others to do so in theirs. These teachers came in for harsh criticism from Jesus: '*And you experts in the Law, woe to you, because you load people down with burdens they can hardly carry, and you yourselves will not lift one finger to help them*' *(Luke 11:46)*. When I look at the teachings of Jesus – the Sermon on the Mount, for example – I realise that with only the Law to help me I will find it impossible to put His teachings into practice in my life. Neither a new law nor a new idealism are enough on their own – I need New Life.

THE NEW LIFE

So what is this New Life? It is life in the Holy Spirit, God at work in and through me. Jesus has supplied the power to live a New Life through His Holy Spirit – I am His channel, His instrument. This means that I rely more on God working in and through me than on my own efforts to grow and to do the right things. It is a completely new principle of life, not just a few adjustments to my old way of life.

If I acknowledge my need and want to have a New Life in the Spirit, then with expectant faith I must ask Him to baptise me in His Holy Spirit. God has promised and He will honour His promise; any barriers to receiving from Him will be with me and not with Him. Baptism in the Spirit is, quite simply, an unconditional surrender to the work of the Spirit in me. It is not a sign of superiority – if anything it underlines my weakness. It is because I am weak that I need and seek God's strength. When He blesses me, I do not myself become stronger by nature; it is simply that God's strength is now flowing more freely in me and through me. But the dangers of human pride will always be lurking in the shadows of my walk in the Spirit. The danger is that instead of constantly acknowledging my natural weakness and humbling myself before God, I can become proud, arrogant, and finally presumptuous in His presence. I think myself without error, above correction – then comes the fall and exclusion from God's blessing.

'APART FROM ME, YOU CAN DO NOTHING'
Baptism in the Spirit is just the beginning. I have learned that as I walk in the Spirit I will make many mistakes, and have failures as well as successes. I must never let the successes make me proud; I must not talk too much about them but must give all the glory to God. But I must never allow my failures to lead me into despair. These too are stepping stones on my journey, not stumbling blocks, and if I am humble I will learn from them. The proud never admit mistakes and so will never learn from them. Above all, I must remember the words of Jesus: *'Apart from me, you can do nothing' (John 15:5)*. St. Paul is an outstanding example of a man who knew his weaknesses

and so relied on God's strength: *'For when I am weak, then I am strong' (2 Corinthians 12:10).* He relied on God's strength and look how God was able to use him! The fact that the Spirit has started the work in me is the guarantee of its completion *(Ephesians 1:14)* provided I remain fully open to this. There must always be a passion for freedom in my heart and an openness to receive from the Spirit. Only then can I be a courageous messenger of the Gospel and a witness to Jesus. It is quite possible to fall out of God's grace and to bring myself back under the Law. This is what happened to the Galatian Christians and we know what Paul said to them: *'You foolish Galatians! After beginning by means of the Spirit, are you now trying to finish by means of the Flesh?' (Galatians 3:1-5).*

CONTRIBUTING TO THE CHURCH'S MISSION

I like the way Pope St. John Paul II explained what it is to be open to the Spirit:

> *'The Spirit is like a wind filling the sails of the great ship of the Church. If, however, we look at her closely, she uses numerous other small sails that are the hearts of the baptized. Everyone, dear friends, is invited to hoist his sail and unfurl it with courage, to permit the Spirit to act with all His sanctifying power. By allowing the Spirit to act in one's own life, one also makes the best contribution to the Church's mission. Do not be afraid to unfurl your sails to the breath of the Spirit!'*

To be baptised in the Spirit is to realise afresh that in

everything I am to live, not out of myself and my own efforts, but out of God's provision of life and power through Christ in the person of the Holy Spirit. I am called to be salt and light so that *'people may see my good deeds and glorify our Father in Heaven' (Matthew 5:13-16)*.

FILLED AND WALKING IN THE SPIRIT
If I am to remain 'salty' and 'light-giving', I need the power of the Holy Spirit to be filling my life.

To be filled with the Spirit is to turn:

1.   From Law to Spirit
2.   From works to Faith
3.   From self to God

To walk in the Spirit is to:

1.   Walk in the love, freedom, and power of God
2.   Listen to the voice and guidance of the Holy Spirit
3.   Do everything in His strength, not in my own
4.   Do it all for the glory of Jesus and my Father in Heaven

When I walk in the will of God, I will have peace and I will know when I divert from His path. Christ died to give me freedom; I need to accept it now and to walk with Him in the power and freedom of His Spirit. Then I'll begin to experience the Spirit-filled life and to hear His voice.

PRAYER AND BIBLE READING
One of the key things that has helped and empowered me over

the years is **the Bible**. After I was baptised in the Spirit, the Lord convinced me that I did not know His Word. So for two years I read it at every opportunity - in fact I read very little else. I loved every minute, and came to a much better understanding of my faith. I realised that I had never really been encouraged to study the Scriptures, and I see this as quite a problem in the Catholic Church. Whenever I have been in a group of Catholics with members of other churches, the difference in Bible knowledge and understanding is often embarrassingly evident. So today I continue to read the Word every day and to reflect upon it in addition to my prayer time, when I sit in the presence of God, listening and waiting upon Him as well as expressing the thoughts and requests in my mind and heart. This is a time when I find the **Gift of Tongues** enormously helpful, as it is so important to practise the daily disciplines of Prayer and Bible reading, and Tongues helps me to keep my concentration. **Archbishop Justin Welby** has publicly said the same thing – he finds the Gift of Tongues really helpful to his personal prayer life on a daily basis.

SURPRISED BY THE SPIRIT!

History has seen too many moves of the Spirit fail when the prophetic vision died and over-organisation strangled their life. If we restrict the Spirit, the gifts will disappear again, as they have in the past. I must let God be God, and do things His way – not mine. This Renewal must remain fully Charismatic, then in thanksgiving for all that has happened and in eager anticipation of all that lies ahead I can say with Paul: *'Now to Him who is able to do immeasurably more than all we ask or imagine, according to His power that is at work within us, to Him be glory in the Church and in Christ Jesus throughout all generations, for ever and ever! Amen (Ephesians 3:20-21).*

Part of this chapter is entitled **'There's Always More!'** and whilst this is absolutely true, how much more there will be depends to a large extent on what I am doing with all that I have already been given. I need to have the basics in place – a life filled with prayer, fed by the Sacraments, and set on fire by the inspiration of the Word of God and the Power of the Spirit. Then there should be endless opportunities to be wonderfully and unexpectedly

SURPRISED BY THE SPIRIT!

TWENTY TWO

A Word from
My Other Half

W E'VE HAD A LOVELY TIME while Charles has been writing this book. Reminiscing, recalling and re-living our time together and being amazed as we realise how often we've been surprised by the Holy Spirit. When we met at Durham University and fell in love, I was an atheist. I had grown up attending our local Presbyterian Church but then, as a teenager, decided to be confirmed in the Church of Wales. Sadly I lost my faith when deciding to read Science at university – after all, who needs a God when science can explain everything? Truly, the arrogance of a teenager. Charles, being Catholic, could have been a problem but that was insignificant compared to the fact that he was English not Welsh!! We managed to overcome the big divide!

It was ten years later when Charles and I had happily married and been blessed with Lucy and Adam that I finally met the Lord. Through meeting some very committed Christians (both Anglicans and Baptists) and seeing Margaret Court (a cradle Catholic) on television giving her testimony of a new relationship with God, that I wondered, maybe for the first time – 'What if I'm wrong and there is a God?' Charles was away so I sat in bed and truly asked God to show me if He existed. I know, very presumptuous – please forgive my arrogance. As I asked Him to show me, I felt a small flame lit in my tummy, which grew larger and larger until I felt engulfed in the flame. It was light and heat and I just said 'That flame you have lit I will never let it go out but I will fan it so that others will see and believe in you as well'. What an honour and privilege that was. The presence of the Holy Spirit was alive in me – and life was going to be different! Charles has already written how he too met our Lord in a fresh way. Isn't God amazing?

So in 1976 we were truly surprised by the Holy Spirit. God is alive and active and the Holy Spirit is living in us enabling us to grow more like Jesus and to know our heavenly Father better. For me, I was surprised to find that God's love in me far surpassed my natural loving feelings. Even my love for Charles became more real – less selfish! Drawing closer to God meant drawing closer to each other. Why was I surprised by that?

A few years after we were baptised in the Spirit, the Lord blessed us with Luke and, three years later Tom, and we found that our care for them was different to that for Lucy and Adam. I think we had always been reasonably good parents and taught Lucy and Adam about Jesus and our Father but it was, for me, more by rote than conviction. But now we parented with the active presence of the Holy Spirit and that certainly changed us, and consequently our family. As Charles has mentioned, we had the added blessing of experiencing God's healing power when Luke, aged four years, was diagnosed as suffering from High Frequency Deafness and yet was healed when John Barr prayed over him. That really encouraged us to have expectant faith. We began to believe that God had plans for us and, if we were willing to listen to Him, we would know what they were. Time and again we would feel the Lord asking us to step out in faith and, as we did, He would open a door before us for our journey to continue.

The Lord builds on nature, that we know, and as we look back we recognise that He has been with us all the time even when we ignored Him. I am so proud of the man I married. He has a greater sense of duty, justice and commitment than anyone I know and is a natural ambassador for God (someone once described him as that!) He has a remarkable ability to enable different groups of people to work together – a truly calming and yet motivating organiser. People visibly relax when he arrives – 'It's OK – Charles is here!' I am so much more of a 'confronter' than he is and I know that he is excellent at damage limitation after some of my outbursts! Above all I am SO grateful that we met and fell in love all those years ago. We really had no idea what was going to happen to us. No idea that God had plans for us. How fortunate we are to have discovered each other and also our loving Father's desire for our happiness! May we continue to walk ever closer with Him and to expect, every day, to be surprised by the Holy Spirit.

> 'May we see Him more clearly,
> love Him more dearly,
> and follow Him more nearly,
> day by day.'
> *(St. Richard of Chichester 1197-1253).*

Sue

Other books by Charles Whitehead

Pentecost is Always for Living
Towards a Fuller Life in the Holy Spirit
Love One Another

available from:
Goodnews Books
www.goodnewsbooks.co.uk
orders@goodnewsbooks.co.uk
01582 571011